Contents

Introduction 2

LESSON 1
Identifying the Main Idea and Details...... 3
Guided Practice.............................5
Independent Practice 7

LESSON 2
Making Predictions.....................12
Guided Practice.............................13
Independent Practice 15

LESSON 3
Recognizing Sequence................. 20
Guided Practice............................. 22
Independent Practice 24

LESSON 4
Comparing and Contrasting 29
Guided Practice............................31
Independent Practice 33

LESSON 5
Identifying Fact and Opinion 38
Guided Practice............................. 40
Independent Practice 42

LESSON 6
Identifying Cause and Effect 47
Guided Practice............................. 49
Independent Practice 51

LESSON 7
Recognizing Author's Purpose.............. 56
Guided Practice............................. 57
Independent Practice 59

LESSON 8
Making Inferences 64
Guided Practice............................. 65
Independent Practice 68

LESSON 9
Drawing Conclusions........................... 73
Guided Practice............................74
Independent Practice 75

LESSON 10
Summarizing................................ 79
Guided Practice............................. 80
Independent Practice 82

LESSON 11
Understanding Plot............................. 87
Guided Practice............................. 89
Independent Practice 90

LESSON 12
Understanding Characters 95
Guided Practice............................. 97
Independent Practice 99

LESSON 13
Using Text Features...........................104
Guided Practice............................106
Independent Practice 108

Glossary 115

Answer Key 120

© HMH Supplemental Publishers Inc.
© Evans Newton, Incorporated

Contents
Reading Intervention, Grade 6

◀ INTRODUCTION

The Steck-Vaughn *Reading Intervention: Foundations for Success* series is designed to help struggling students master foundational reading skills. Each workbook provides practice with key reading comprehension skills and other literacy skills. The passages in each workbook cover a wide range of high-interest topics and include both fiction and nonfiction texts with low readability levels so students are able to focus on skill development.

Each workbook contains 13 lessons. Each lesson is supported by the following activity pages.

• **Introduction to the Skill** explains the reading comprehension skill

• **Guided Practice** provides a reading passage with interactive reader response questions that target the reading comprehension skill

• **Independent Practice** provides vocabulary support, a reading passage, and comprehension questions

Introduction to the Skill
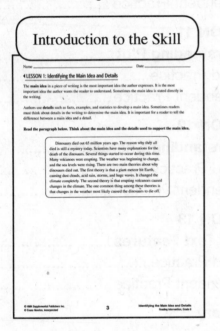

Guided Practice
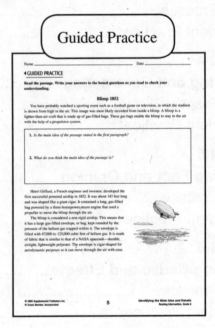

Independent Practice
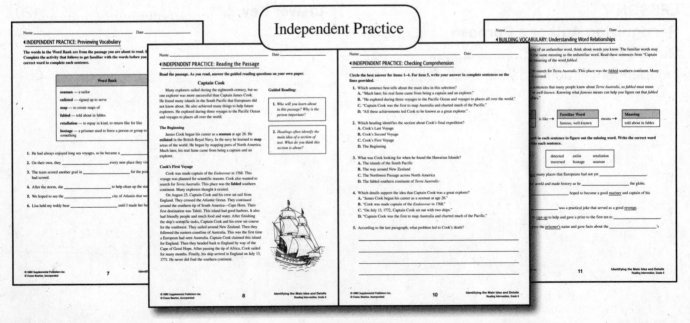

◀ LESSON 1: Identifying the Main Idea and Details

The **main idea** in a piece of writing is the most important idea the author expresses. It is the most important idea the author wants the reader to understand. Sometimes the main idea is stated directly in the writing.

Authors use **details** such as facts, examples, and statistics to develop a main idea. Sometimes readers must think about details in the writing to determine the main idea. It is important for a reader to tell the difference between a main idea and a detail.

Read the paragraph below. Think about the main idea and the details used to support the main idea.

Dinosaurs died out 65 million years ago. The reason why they all died is still a mystery today. Scientists have many explanations for the death of the dinosaurs. Several things started to occur during this time. Many volcanoes were erupting. The weather was beginning to change, and the sea levels were rising. There are two main theories about why dinosaurs died out. The first theory is that a giant meteor hit Earth, causing dust clouds, acid rain, storms, and huge waves. It changed the climate completely. The second theory is that erupting volcanoes caused changes in the climate. The one common thing among these theories is that changes in the weather most likely caused the dinosaurs to die off.

1. Think about what the paragraph is mainly about. What is the main idea the author writes about? Write your answer in the Main Idea box.

2. Think about how the author develops the main idea. What details does the author use to develop the main idea? Write your answers in the circles.

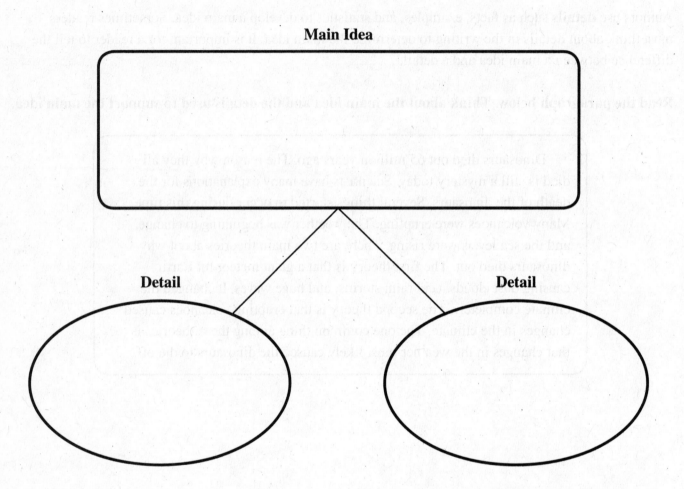

Main Idea

Detail

Detail

Name _____ Date _____

Read the passage. Write your answers to the boxed questions as you read to check your understanding.

Blimp 1852

You have probably watched a sporting event such as a football game on television, in which the stadium is shown from high in the air. This image was most likely recorded from inside a blimp. A blimp is a lighter-than-air craft that is made up of gas-filled bags. These gas bags enable the blimp to stay in the air with the help of a propulsion system.

---

1. *Is the main idea of the passage stated in the first paragraph?*

2. *What do you think the main idea of the passage is?*

Henri Giffard, a French engineer and inventor, developed the first successful powered airship in 1852. It was about 143 feet long and was shaped like a giant cigar. It contained a long, gas-filled bag powered by a three-horsepower steam engine that used a propeller to move the blimp through the air.

The blimp is considered a non-rigid airship. This means that it has a large gas-filled envelope, or bag, kept rounded by the pressure of the helium gas trapped within it. The envelope is filled with 67,000 to 125,000 cubic feet of helium gas. It is made of fabric that is similar to that of a NASA spacesuit—durable, airtight, lightweight polyester. The envelope is cigar-shaped for aerodynamic purposes so it can move through the air with ease.

3. *What details does the author include to develop the main idea?*

A blimp is capable of flying and hovering without expending much fuel or energy. Using its two 200- to 400-horsepower engines, it can stay aloft for many hours and into many days. Because of these reasons, a blimp is ideal for (and is mostly used for) recording sporting events, providing advertising for companies such as Goodyear, Fuji, and Metropolitan Life Insurance, and scientific matters such as tracking the movement of whale pods in the ocean.

4. *Now that you have finished reading, what do you think the main idea of this passage is?*

5. *List three details the author uses to develop the main idea.*

◄ INDEPENDENT PRACTICE: Previewing Vocabulary

The words in the Word Bank are from the passage you are about to read. Study the definitions. Complete the activity that follows to get familiar with the words before you begin reading. Write the correct word to complete each sentence.

Word Bank
seaman — a sailor
enlisted — signed up to serve
map — to create maps of
fabled — told about in fables
retaliation — to repay in kind, to return like for like
hostage — a prisoner used to force a person or group to do something

1. He had always enjoyed long sea voyages, so he became a _____.

2. On their own, they _____ every new place they visit.

3. The team scored another goal in _____ for the point the other team had scored.

4. After the storm, she _____ to help clean up the state park.

5. We hoped to see the _____ city of Atlantis that we had read about.

6. Lisa held my teddy bear _____ until I made her bed.

◀ INDEPENDENT PRACTICE: Reading the Passage

Read the passage. As you read, answer the guided reading questions on your own paper.

Captain Cook

Many explorers sailed during the eighteenth century, but no one explorer was more successful than Captain James Cook. He found many islands in the South Pacific that Europeans did not know about. He also achieved many things to help future explorers. He explored during three voyages to the Pacific Ocean and voyages to places all over the world.

The Beginning

James Cook began his career as a **seaman** at age 26. He **enlisted** in the British Royal Navy. In the navy he learned to **map** areas of the world. He began by mapping parts of North America. Much later, his real fame came from being a captain and an explorer.

Cook's First Voyage

Cook was made captain of the *Endeavour* in 1768. This voyage was planned for scientific reasons. Cook also wanted to search for *Terra Australis*. This place was the **fabled** southern continent. Many explorers thought it existed.

On August 25, Captain Cook and his crew set sail from England. They crossed the Atlantic Ocean. They continued around the southern tip of South America—Cape Horn. Their first destination was Tahiti. This island had good harbors. It also had friendly people and much food and water. After finishing the ship's scientific tasks, Captain Cook and his crew set course for the southwest. They sailed around New Zealand. Then they followed the eastern coastline of Australia. This was the first time a European had seen Australia. Captain Cook claimed this island for England. Then they headed back to England by way of the Cape of Good Hope. After passing the tip of Africa, Cook sailed for many months. Finally, his ship arrived in England on July 13, 1771. He never did find the southern continent.

Guided Reading:

1. *Who will you learn about in this passage? Why is the person important?*

2. *Headings often identify the main idea of a section of text. What do you think this section is about?*

Cook's Second Voyage

On July 13, 1772, Captain Cook set out with two ships. These ships were the *Resolution* and the *Adventure*. Cook and his crew sailed around the Cape of Good Hope. Then they went south into the Antarctic Ocean. In January 1773, they crossed the Antarctic Circle. They could not continue to Antarctica because ice blocked the route, so Cook decided to sail north to warmer waters. They sailed to Tahiti. After leaving this island, Cook found and explored many islands in the South Pacific. Easter Island, Vanuatu (say *van oo AW too*), and the Marquesas (say *mar KAY saws*) were a few of these islands. After over three years at sea, Captain Cook and his crew returned to England. They reached home on July 29, 1775.

Cook's Last Voyage

During this voyage, Cook wanted to find the Northwest Passage. This passage was thought to be a way across North America. Cook and his crew set out in the *Resolution*. Its sister ship, the *Discovery*, came with them. During this expedition, Cook found the Hawaiian Islands. The native people of Hawaii thought Captain Cook was a god. After staying awhile, Cook and his crew sailed north up to Alaska and through the Bering Strait. Cook concluded that there was no Northwest Passage. They turned around and went back to Hawaii. When they arrived there, things had changed. Cook discovered that they had worn out their welcome. This led to the native people stealing one of the ships. In **retaliation**, Cook took a Hawaiian chief **hostage**. The native people became angry and surrounded Cook and his crew. Cook was killed on February 14, 1779. The crew returned to England without Cook and arrived home on October 4, 1780.

Captain Cook was the first to map Australia and charted much of the Pacific. He also found many islands that Europeans did not know about and proved that there was no Northwest Passage. All these achievements led Cook to be known as a great explorer.

Guided Reading:

3. *Read the heading. What do you think this section is about?*

4. *What is the stated main idea of this section?*

Name _____ Date _____

◀ INDEPENDENT PRACTICE: Checking Comprehension

Circle the best answer for items 1–4. For item 5, write your answer in complete sentences on the lines provided.

1. Which sentence best tells about the main idea in this selection?

   A. "Much later, his real fame came from being a captain and an explorer."

   B. "He explored during three voyages to the Pacific Ocean and voyages to places all over the world."

   C. "Captain Cook was the first to map Australia and charted much of the Pacific."

   D. "All these achievements led Cook to be known as a great explorer."

2. Which heading identifies the section about Cook's final expedition?

   A. Cook's Last Voyage

   B. Cook's Second Voyage

   C. Cook's First Voyage

   D. The Beginning

3. What was Cook looking for when he found the Hawaiian Islands?

   A. The islands of the South Pacific

   B. The way around New Zealand

   C. The Northwest Passage across North America

   D. The fabled southern continent of *Terra Australis*

4. Which details support the idea that Captain Cook was a great explorer?

   A. "James Cook began his career as a seaman at age 26."

   B. "Cook was made captain of the *Endeavour* in 1768."

   C. "On July 13, 1772, Captain Cook set out with two ships."

   D. "Captain Cook was the first to map Australia and charted much of the Pacific."

5. According to the last paragraph, what problem led to Cook's death?

   _____

   _____

   _____

   _____

◀ BUILDING VOCABULARY: Understanding Word Relationships

To figure out the meaning of an unfamiliar word, think about words you know. The familiar words may have the same or nearly the same meaning as the unfamiliar word. Read these sentences from "Captain Cook." Think about the meaning of the word *fabled*.

> Cook also wanted to search for *Terra Australis*. This place was the <u>fabled</u> southern continent. Many explorers thought it existed.

You can tell from these sentences that many people knew about *Terra Australis*, so *fabled* must mean something like *famous* or *well-known*. Knowing what *famous* means can help you figure out that *fabled* means "told about in fables."

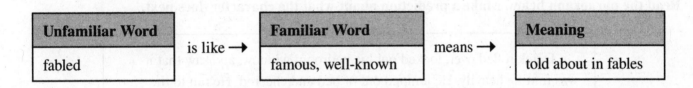

Unfamiliar Word		**Familiar Word**		**Meaning**
fabled	is like →	famous, well-known	means →	told about in fables

Use the underlined word in each sentence to figure out the missing word. Write the correct word from the box to complete each sentence.

detected	enlist	retaliation
traversed	hostage	seaman

1. Captain Cook <u>found</u> many places that Europeans had not yet _____.

2. He <u>crisscrossed</u> the world and made history as he _____ the globe.

3. The young _____ hoped to become a good <u>mariner</u> and captain of his own ship.

4. Her _____ was a practical joke that served as a good <u>revenge</u>.

5. We asked parents to <u>sign up</u> to help and gave a prize to the first ten to _____.

6. The news anchor gave the <u>prisoner's</u> name and gave facts about the _____'s life.

◄ LESSON 2: Making Predictions

A **prediction** is a kind of guess about the future. When you make a statement about what may happen tomorrow or next year or in ten years, you are making a prediction.

While reading, readers often **make predictions** about what comes next. They wonder what happens next in a story and make a guess. They think about what comes next in a text and read on to find out. Readers use details and information they have read to predict about something they have <u>not</u> read yet. They use information they already know, too.

Think about a story or text that you are reading. What has happened in the story so far? What do you think happens next? What information have you read in the text? What information do you think comes next?

Read the paragraph below. Make a prediction about what the character does next.

> Derek rolled over, looked out his bedroom window, and saw that it was raining heavily. He jumped out of bed and cheered. He ran to the other window and looked out at the rain again. It looked as though it would keep raining for a long time, maybe forever. Derek grinned with delight.

Read the graphic organizer below. It tells what Derek has done so far.
Make a prediction about what happens next. Write your prediction on the lines.

| Derek sees that it is raining. | Derek jumps out of bed, cheers, and grins. | It looks like it might rain for a long time. | _____ _____ _____ |

◀ **GUIDED PRACTICE**

Read the passage. Write your answers to the boxed questions as you read to check your understanding.

My Aunt Julia

Aunt Julia believed that the people in her neighborhood didn't deserve the eyesore. Three huge buildings had been knocked down, and the workers had not completely cleaned up the area. She decided to do something about it.

First, Aunt Julia made some phone calls to find out who owned the land where the buildings had been knocked down. It belonged to the city, she learned. Next, she called the mayor's office to find out what he would do to clean it up. The mayor wasn't in, but his assistant told her that the city had big plans for the property.

"I felt like he was patting me on the head," she told me later.

---

1. *What is Aunt Julia doing?*

2. *What do you predict Aunt Julia does next? Make a prediction.*

Weeks passed. Aunt Julia waited patiently. Nothing happened. Instead of giving up, Aunt Julia decided this time she would write a friendly letter to the mayor asking for action. She knew that sometimes you had to keep trying if you wanted to succeed.

---

3. *Aunt Julia has done even more. What do you predict happens next in the passage?*

The mayor's office did not call or write her at all. Months went by, and still nothing happened. Now Aunt Julia was even more determined. She called the local newspaper.

The newspaper wrote a front-page article about how the mayor had done nothing to fix up the block in Aunt Julia's neighborhood. Within a week, all the garbage and concrete and metal was carried off. The ugly fence came down.

---

4. *Think about the predictions you made. Was each of them correct? Were any of them incorrect? How do you know?*

Name _____ Date _____

◄ **INDEPENDENT PRACTICE: Previewing Vocabulary**

The words in the Word Bank are from the passage you are about to read. Study the definitions. Complete the activity that follows to get familiar with the words before you begin reading. Write the correct word to complete each sentence.

Word Bank
shrubs — plants with branches close to the ground
weeded — cleared weeds
store — to put away and keep
groggily — in a sleepy and confused way
culprit — the person who is guilty of doing something

1. In the spring, I helped Grandpa _____ the winter gear in the attic.

2. Then we _____ the garden plot to get it ready for planting the vegetable garden.

3. "It's too early to plant seeds, Grandpa," I mumbled _____ at dawn the next morning.

4. Later, we trimmed the bushes and _____ by the fence.

5. Grandma found muddy footprints on the porch. She asked which of us was the

   _____.

◄ INDEPENDENT PRACTICE: Reading the Passage

Read the passage. As you read, answer the guided reading questions on your own paper.

The Great Refrigerator Mystery

A mystery can happen anywhere, even in a kid's house. Let me tell you about a mystery that happened last summer in my house. It was just after my baby sister was born.

My mom and dad were waking up every two hours to feed the baby. My Grandma Ana had come to stay with us for a few weeks. She was supposed to help with the new baby, but she didn't really.

"She doesn't like taking care of babies much," Mom said.

Grandma Ana planted **shrubs** and painted the fence. She **weeded** the garden and mowed the lawn. She loved making things and fixing things, but she always left behind a mess that my parents had to clean up. Best of all, she took my younger brother and me to the movies and baseball games and to this kids' gym that had a climbing wall.

The morning after Grandma Ana arrived, Mom opened the refrigerator and found my little brother's toy police cars on a shelf. "Which one of you boys put these in the refrigerator?" she asked. "They were in the baby stroller yesterday. And where did the baby's bottle go? I put a bottle in here for her, and now I can't find it. Richard? Do you know anything about this?"

"Huh?" Dad was holding the baby at the kitchen table. He was dressed for work, but he looked half asleep. "This coffee isn't helping me much."

"You're wearing different colored socks again," Grandma Ana said.

When Mom got out the stroller to walk me to the bus stop, the missing bottle was in the seat.

The next morning was Saturday. "Why aren't you dressed?" Dad cried when he saw me. "You'll miss the bus! You'll be late for school!"

"It's Saturday, Richard," Mom said calmly, opening the refrigerator. Then she exclaimed, "There's a bottle of laundry detergent in here! And the milk is gone. There was a whole gallon of milk in here last night. How can we lose a gallon of milk?"

Mom found the milk when she went downstairs to start a load of laundry. It was on the shelf where the detergent usually was. From then on, things got worse.

Guided Reading:

1. *What prediction can you make about what Grandma Ana does instead of helping with the new baby?*

2. *Make a prediction about who knows the answers to Mom's questions.*

3. *What prediction can you make about how things got worse?*

The next morning, there was a baseball glove in the refrigerator and a pound of butter in the bin where we store sports equipment. By then, I had recognized the pattern. When Mom found a paint can and a paintbrush in the refrigerator, I went right down to the shelf in the basement where we keep our paints and found the orange juice. I also found a bottle of soy sauce and a package of hot dog buns there.

"How did those things end up in the refrigerator?" Dad asked **groggily**, opening the back door.

"What are you doing, Richard? You can't go to work looking like that. Your shirt's still unbuttoned."

"What? I'm sure I remember buttoning it."

"How long were you awake with the baby last night?"

"I couldn't go back to sleep, so I went around the house, picking up after your mother and the boys."

When Dad left for work, I informed Mom that I had the solution to the mystery. All I needed was a sleeping bag and a flashlight to prove who the **culprit** was.

That night, I spread out my bag under the kitchen table. The baby cried at about midnight, and Dad came into the kitchen to warm up a bottle.

I must have fallen back asleep because what woke me up next was the clink-clank sound as Dad put a bicycle helmet into the refrigerator. I watched him shuffle down the basement stairs in his slippers, carrying a package of cheese sticks and a box of squeezable yogurts to put next to my bicycle.

After that, Mom let Dad sleep through the night for a whole week. And every evening before bedtime, Grandma Ana, my brother, and I picked up all of our things. The case of the great refrigerator mystery was closed.

Guided Reading:

4. *What prediction can you make about how the great refrigerator mystery is solved?*

◄ INDEPENDENT PRACTICE: Checking Comprehension

Circle the best answer for items 1–4. For item 5, write your answer in complete sentences on the lines provided.

1. At the beginning of the passage, a good prediction to make about Grandma Ana is that she is —
   A. very smart
   B. helpful
   C. loving
   D. fun

2. What prediction can you make about what the narrator of the passage will be like when he is an adult?
   A. He will be a funny dad.
   B. He will tell sad stories.
   C. He will live with his parents.
   D. He will become a detective.

3. Which is a good prediction of who the culprit is?
   A. Grandma Ana because she doesn't normally live there
   B. Mom because she finds odd things in the refrigerator
   C. The two sons because they are young children
   D. Dad because he has to go to work

4. If Dad does not get enough sleep again, what do you think will happen?
   A. Mom will get a full-time job outside the home.
   B. Grandma Ana will stop cleaning up after herself.
   C. Strange things will start appearing in the refrigerator.
   D. The two sons will go to the movies and baseball games.

5. Which part of the setting is most important to the conflict? Explain why.

   _____

   _____

   _____

◀ BUILDING VOCABULARY: Using Antonyms

When we talk about antonyms, we are talking about words that have opposite or nearly opposite meanings. Authors sometimes use antonyms to explore an idea by telling what something is *not*.

Readers can use antonyms to better understand what they read, such as to determine the meaning of an unfamiliar word. The reader can check to see if a word with an obviously opposite meaning is nearby. Look at the underlined antonyms in this sentence from the passage.

She loved making things and fixing things, but she always left behind a <u>mess</u> *that my parents had to* <u>clean up</u>*.*

Knowing what <u>clean up</u> means helps you understand the meaning of <u>mess</u>.

Write the pair of antonyms in each sentence.

1. The good guy was not the culprit of the passage.

   _____

2. We all worked to find a solution to the mystery.

   _____

3. After drinking a cup of coffee, she was wide-awake and no longer groggy.

   _____

4. The band director asked the band members to store the musical instruments; however, the band members misunderstood him and thought he wanted them to display the instruments.

   _____

5. After a sleepless night, my kind friend turned into a grim person.

   _____

◀ LESSON 3: Recognizing Sequence

When we talk about the **sequence** in a text, we are referring to the order in which actions or events happen. It is important to identify the sequence in a text to know what happens and to better understand the text, the characters and their actions, and why things happen as they do.

Authors use signal words such as *first*, *next*, *later*, *so*, and *then* as they tell events. These words help readers identify the sequence in a text. When you read sentences, look for signal words to help you recognize sequence.

Read the paragraph below. Think about what happened and when it happened. Look for signal words to help you recognize sequence.

> Mother Teresa was born in 1910. She was born in Skopje, Yugoslavia. At age 12, she already knew she wanted to be a missionary. She wished to help people. First, she joined the Sisters of Loreto at age 18. This order of nuns did missions in India. Next, at age 20, she officially became a nun. Then she went to Calcutta. From 1931 to 1948, she taught high school. However, after seeing the suffering in the streets, she left teaching to work with the poor in the slums. Later, in 1950, she started her own order of nuns. The Missionaries of Charity looked after those who were not wanted. Mother Teresa opened many orphanages. She has been given many awards for her work. She died in 1997 still doing what she was called to do—help others.

Name _____ Date _____

Write the sequence of events in Mother Teresa's life on the graphic organizer below.

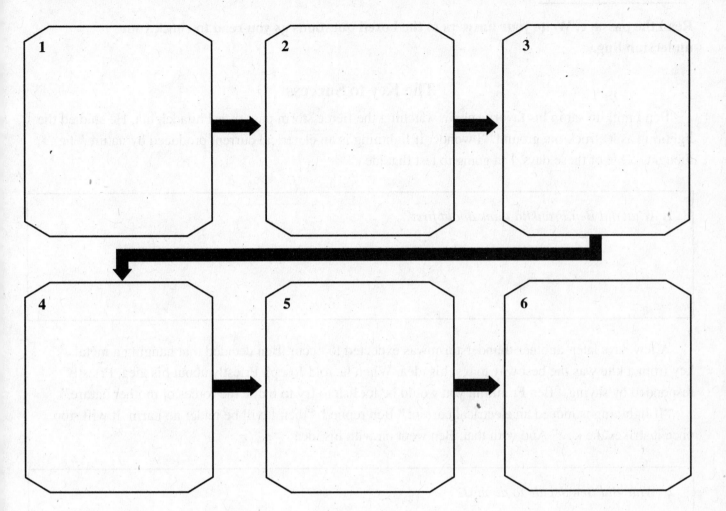

◀ **GUIDED PRACTICE**

Read the passage. Write your answers to the boxed questions as you read to check your understanding.

The Key to Success

Ben Franklin sat in his favorite chair, watching the fierce storm pass over Philadelphia. He studied the lightning as it struck the ground. "I wonder if lightning is an electrical current produced by nature," he thought. "One of these days, I'm going to test that idea."

---

1. *What did Ben Franklin think about first?*

A few days later, another thunderstorm was expected to occur. Ben decided that hanging a metal key from a kite was the best way to test his idea. When he told Joseph Priestly about his idea, Priestly responded by saying, "Ben Franklin, you would be foolish to try to battle the forces of mother nature."

"If lightning is indeed an electrical current," Ben replied, "then I will be under no harm. It will stop once it strikes the key." And with that, Ben went on with his idea.

---

2. *What did Ben decide to do next?*

Once Ben had attached the key to the kite, he began to allow the wind to take the kite high in the sky. He waited and waited. Finally, a promising storm cloud was directly over the kite. However, it passed by without letting out one lightning strike. Soon Ben noticed some pieces of the string standing straight up. Seeing this, Ben gently touched his knuckle against the key, and an electrical spark appeared.

3. *Then what happened?*

"Hurrah!" Ben yelled. "My theory was accurate. Lightning is electrical current."

Ben Franklin became the first person from the United States to prove the existence of electricity in nature.

4. *What did Ben Franklin learn in the end?*

◄ INDEPENDENT PRACTICE: Previewing Vocabulary

The words in the Word Bank are from the passage you are about to read. Study the definitions. Complete the activity that follows to get familiar with the words before you begin reading. Write the letter of the correct word that completes each sentence.

Word Bank

canal — a channel of water

isthmus — a small strip of land connecting two larger land bodies

waterway — a long body of water for boats to travel on

terrain — ground or land

locks — water-filled chambers of a canal closed off with gates and used to change the water level

treaty — an agreement between countries or governments

landslides — soil and rock that falls off and slides down slopes

---

1. The farmers built a _____ to get lake water.

2. The two states were separated only by the _____.

3. There were many _____ after the spring rains.

4. Ship passengers enjoy watching how the canal's _____ work.

5. The _____ was signed by the presidents of three countries.

6. We hiked over rough _____ to reach the peak.

7. Huge ships can travel through the _____ of the Great Lakes.

a. locks

b. terrain

c. canal

d. waterways

e. treaty

f. isthmus

g. landslides

◀ INDEPENDENT PRACTICE: Reading the Passage

Read the passage. As you read, answer the guided reading questions on your own paper.

Built Across Land

For centuries, sailing from the Pacific Ocean to the Atlantic Ocean was difficult. The trip from ocean to ocean took many months. The route was far around the southern tip of South America. Sailors from around the world wanted to build a **canal** across a small country named Panama. With a canal across Panama, sailing between these oceans would be quicker and easier.

One part of Panama was only about 35 miles across, so it was the best location for a canal. Still, it wasn't until the late 1800s that digging and building a canal over land would actually be done. At long last, between 1904 and 1914, the United States built the canal. The dream of many sailors had finally come true.

The Panama Canal cuts across the **Isthmus** of Panama. It allows ships to travel between the Pacific and Atlantic oceans. This **waterway** passes through Panama. It stretches across about 35 miles of hilly **terrain**. It is made up of natural and man-made lakes, channels, and a series of **locks** used to help ships move from one ocean to the other. How the Panama Canal was built is a long story.

For many years, even decades, many people in the United States had wanted to build a canal. They wanted to build it somewhere across Central America. They considered both Nicaragua and Panama. It was determined that Panama was the better place, so in 1902, the U.S. Congress and President Theodore Roosevelt decided to build the Panama Canal. They signed a treaty with Colombia. At that time, Panama was under the rule of Colombia, and the **treaty** was rejected.

Panamanians really wanted the canal built in their country, and in 1903, they declared Panama's independence from Colombia. They no longer wanted to be under Colombian rule. The United States supported the revolution. Soon afterward, the United States signed a treaty with Panama. In the treaty, Panama gave consent for the United States to build the canal, and the United States purchased a strip of land across the middle of the isthmus. They were ready to build the canal.

Construction on the canal began in 1904. Independent contractors did most of the digging and building. In all, 100,000

Guided Reading:

1. *How did sailors travel from the Pacific Ocean to the Atlantic Ocean before the Panama Canal was built?*

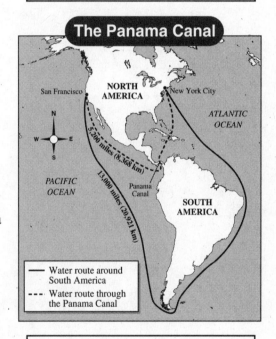

The Panama Canal

— Water route around South America

--- Water route through the Panama Canal

2. *What happened before building of the canal began?*

3. *Which sequence signal word does the author use in this paragraph?*

4. *When did the building of the Panama Canal begin?*

people moved to Panama. They moved there from all over the world. They did this so they could work on the canal.

Finally, the Panama Canal was completed in 1914. The first ship sailed through on August 15 of that year. But in 1915, the canal was closed. It was shut down because of **landslides**. The canal had become too dangerous. Then World War I began. The war delayed the official opening of the canal for over five years. The Panama Canal officially opened in 1920. Since its opening, it has served ships from all over the world. And today, work is under way to widen the Panama Canal to fit larger ships!

Guided Reading:

5. *When did the building of the Panama Canal end?*

◀ INDEPENDENT PRACTICE: Checking Comprehension

Circle the best answer for items 1–4. For item 5, write your answer in complete sentences on the lines provided.

1. Which sentence from the passage tells what happened first in the building of the Panama Canal?
   A. "The Panama Canal officially opened in 1920."
   B. "The first ship sailed through on August 15 of that year."
   C. "At long last, between 1904 and 1914, the United States built the canal."
   D. "Sailors from around the world wanted to build a canal across a small country named Panama."

2. What happened <u>last</u> in the building of the Panama Canal?
   A. A treaty with Colombia was rejected.
   B. The Panama Canal officially opened.
   C. A great many people moved to Panama.
   D. Panama gained independence from Colombia.

3. In what order did the events below occur?
   A. A need was determined. Then a plan was made, and a treaty was signed. Lastly, a canal was built.
   B. A plan was made, and a need was determined. Then a treaty was signed, and a canal was built.
   C. A treaty was signed before a need was determined. Then a plan was made, and a canal was built.
   D. A treaty was signed, and then a plan was made. A need was determined. Then a canal was built.

4. Which years are part of the sequence of events in building the Panama Canal?
   A. The 1800s
   B. 1902 and 1903
   C. 1904 to 1914
   D. 1915 and 1920

5. Recall the building of the Panama Canal. Write the sequence of the events in your own words.

   _____

   _____

   _____

   _____

◀ BUILDING VOCABULARY: Using Synonyms

Synonyms are words that have the same or nearly the same meaning. Authors use synonyms in their writing to avoid repeating a word or words. Using synonyms helps to make a text more interesting. Readers can use synonyms to determine the meaning of unfamiliar words and to better understand what they read.

Decide which vocabulary word in the box means the same or almost the same as the underlined word or phrase. Write the word on the line provided.

canal	waterway	locks	landslides
isthmus	terrain	treaty	

1. The <u>avalanches</u> interrupted the use of the canal.

   _____

2. Huge ships carry cargo through the <u>shipping channel</u>.

   _____

3. Two strong <u>gates</u> keep the ships still while the water level changes.

   _____

4. Several countries have a <u>channel of water</u> for helping people and materials get around.

   _____

5. The governments of several countries signed the <u>agreement</u> about the purchase.

   _____

6. Many people travel across this <u>narrow strip of land</u> between one ocean and another.

   _____

7. We studied the <u>geography</u> of the land before setting out on our journey.

   _____

◄ LESSON 4: Comparing and Contrasting

One way to think about what you are reading is to **compare and contrast** pieces of information. Compare information by finding what is similar about two or more people, places, things, animals, objects, or ideas presented in the text. Contrast information by determining their differences.

You can compare and contrast two or more pieces of writing, or you can compare and contrast certain elements found in a single piece of writing. Are you wondering how to find what is similar and different between people, places, things, animals, objects, or ideas in a text? It's easy. Find information about each of them and then determine if the pieces of information are similar or different in any way. Just remember: compare what is similar, contrast what is different.

Read the paragraph below. Compare and contrast pieces of information.

> Some may think that alligators and crocodiles are the same. They are very different in many ways, but the differences are hard to see. One difference is the shape of their heads. Alligators have a wider, more rounded head. Crocs have a more pointed, narrow head. Since a croc's head is narrow, some of its teeth are visible when its mouth is closed. An alligator's teeth fit nicely in sockets in its mouth. Its teeth are visible only when its mouth is open. Another difference is that alligators prefer to stay in fresh water. Crocodiles have no problem venturing into either salt or fresh water. There are some kinds of crocs that live in salt water.

Name _____ Date _____

1. Think about the pieces of information in the paragraph about alligators and crocodiles that are similar and different. Underline the sentences that contrast the animals' heads. Write these differences on the graphic organizer below.

2. Think about other pieces of information. Are they similar? Are they different? Write your answers on the graphic organizer below.

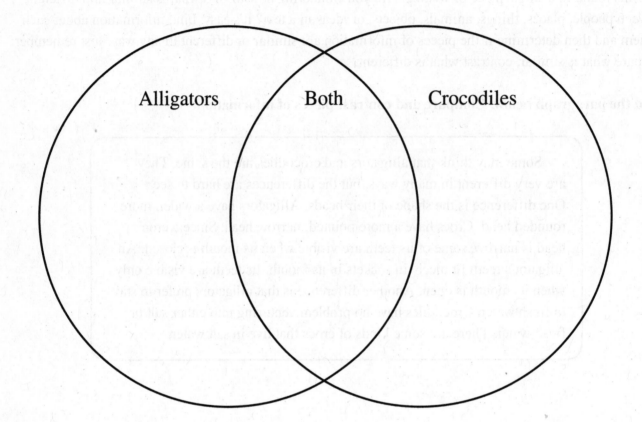

Alligators   Both   Crocodiles

Name _____   Date _____

Read the passage. Write your answers to the boxed questions as you read to check your understanding.

Two Lizards

There are many kinds of lizards in the world. Two of the most interesting are the basilisk and the anole.

Basilisk

These lizards live in trees and rocks near the water. They live in tropical areas. The most amazing thing about these lizards is that they can run on water for a short time. Their legs and their tail help them achieve this. Their back feet have special scales that also help them run on water. Basilisks are green or brown in color. They are 2 to 2½ feet long and eat insects, spiders, and worms.

Basilisks live in the tropical rain forests of South America.

---

1. *Describe the body of a basilisk.*

2. *What is one amazing thing about basilisks?*

Anole

There are two kinds of this lizard: the green anole and the brown anole. They like to live in tropical areas and can be found in the southeastern part of the United States. Anoles are found in bushes and trees and on rock walls and houses. They like to sit in the warm sun. Anoles can be up to nine inches long and like to eat insects and spiders.

3. *What do anoles look like?*

4. *Where in nature do anoles live?*

In the United States, most anoles are found in Florida.

5. *Compare and contrast basilisks and anoles.*

Name _____ Date _____

The words in the Word Bank are from the passage you are about to read. Study the definitions. Complete the activity that follows to get familiar with the words before you begin reading. Write the letter of the sentence that uses the word from the Word Bank correctly.

Word Bank

eyesight — ability to see

molars — big teeth in the back of the mouth used for grinding food

upright — in a vertical or straight up position

nutritional — full of nutrients for living and growing

marsupial — a type of mammal that has an outer pouch for carrying its young

sensitive — able to smell, hear, taste, feel, or see very well

nocturnal — active at nighttime

_____ **1. a.** The story was filled with excitement and nutritional adventures.
　　　　　b. The nutritional information is written on the side of the cereal box.

_____ **2. a.** The nocturnal hamster played in the cage all night.
　　　　　b. Humans are nocturnal animals, so they are alert during the day.

_____ **3. a.** He felt the silk with his sensitive fingers.
　　　　　b. Her shoes were sensitive from being worn so much.

_____ **4. a.** The fable ends with a molar about kindness.
　　　　　b. Many animals chew with their large molars.

_____ **5. a.** He sat upright at the sound of the alarm clock.
　　　　　b. At the school dance, the boys were nervous and upright.

_____ **6. a.** I closed my eyes to show her the freckle on my eyesight.
　　　　　b. Owls generally have very good eyesight.

_____ **7. a.** The kangaroo is a marsupial.
　　　　　b. The shark is a marsupial.

Name _____ Date _____

◀ INDEPENDENT PRACTICE: Reading the Passage

Read the passage. As you read, answer the guided reading questions on your own paper.

From China to Australia

Giant Pandas

Giant pandas live in the mountain ranges of central China. They are found mostly in forests that contain bamboo. They are solitary animals, which means they mostly live alone. But pandas have been known to share their territory with a small group of other pandas.

The shape of a panda's body is similar to those of other bears, but pandas' bodies are covered in black-and-white fur. Black fur covers their ears, legs, and shoulders, and surrounds their eyes. The rest of their fur is white. Pandas' fur is thick and wooly. It helps protect them from the weather.

Pandas grow to be 4 to 6 feet long. They can weigh up to 250 pounds. Their **eyesight** is very good, and they have sharp front teeth. These teeth help them bite off stalks of bamboo, which is mostly what they eat. Their large **molars** and strong jaws help crush the bamboo. Ninety percent of their food comes from bamboo, which makes them primarily herbivores, or plant-eating animals. They eat sitting **upright**, holding the food with their front paws. Since bamboo is low in **nutritional** value and is hard to digest, pandas eat 20 to 40 pounds of it per day. However, pandas do not need to drink much water. They get much of the water their bodies need from the bamboo they eat. Not only do they use their paws for eating, but they also use them for climbing trees. Pandas are good climbers. Their paws have five clawed fingers that help them grip the sides of a tree. They are sometimes seen napping high in the trees.

Panda cubs are born pink, hairless, and blind. They weigh about four ounces and are about the size of a stick of butter. They usually stay with their mother for about two years.

Pandas communicate with other pandas in many ways. They leave scent marks on trees and have eleven different calls for the occasional meetings with other pandas. They do not roar like other bears, or hibernate for that matter. Their call is more of a bleat like the sound made by sheep or goats.

Pandas are cute and cuddly looking. But they can be dangerous, even though they are a symbol of peace.

Guided Reading:

1. *How is the black fur on pandas different from the white fur?*

2. *How are pandas different from other bears?*

Koalas

Koalas are thought to look like living teddy bears. But this small, bearlike animal is not even a bear. It is a **marsupial**, like a kangaroo. Koalas live in Australia. They are found mostly in the tall eucalyptus-tree forests in the eastern part of the country. However, some are also found along the coastal regions and low woodland areas. Koalas are tree-dwelling animals, which means they live only in trees.

Koalas are ash gray in color with tinges of brown in their fur. Their fur protects them from the weather. It keeps them cool in the summer and warm in the winter. Koalas grow to weigh about 20 pounds and are usually 24 to 33 inches in length. They have paws with five digits, each of which has a long, sharp claw. These claws enable them to climb trees with ease and grasp their food while eating.

The koalas' diet consists entirely of leaves of eucalyptus (yoo ka lip tis), or gum, trees. This means they are herbivores. The koala's nose has **sensitive** hairs that help it find the best-tasting eucalyptus leaves. Each day a koala eats 2.5 pounds of eucalyptus leaves. Koalas are very picky eaters, however, and only eat the moist tender tips of the leaves. Their sharp front teeth help them nip the leaves from branches, while their molars help crush the gum leaves.

Koalas are **nocturnal** animals. This means they are active only at night and during the dawn and dusk hours. They actually sleep about 18 hours per day to conserve energy. Some koalas may stay in the same tree for many days.

Koalas live in societies like humans do. They share their "home range" territory with other koalas. To communicate, koalas use different types of calls. They make grunting noises when angry. They may scream and shake when scared. Mothers and babies communicate with soft clicking noises, squeaking sounds, and humming and murmuring. Koalas also mark trees with their scent.

Koalas may look like cuddly teddy bears. In reality, they are more like kangaroos that don't hop or opossums that don't hang upside down by a tail.

Guided Reading:

3. *How are koalas' and pandas' fur the same? In what similar way do pandas and koalas use their claws?*

4. *Contrast the diet of koalas and pandas.*

5. *Describe the similarities in how pandas and koalas communicate.*

◀ **INDEPENDENT PRACTICE: Checking Comprehension**

Circle the best answer for items 1–4. For item 5, write your answer in complete sentences on the lines provided.

1. Which details from the passage can you compare?
   A. That pandas do not behave like bears
   B. That pandas and koalas leave scent marks
   C. The length that pandas and koalas grow
   D. The amount of water pandas and koalas drink

2. Pandas and koalas are similar in that they —
   A. use their claws to climb
   B. roar like bears do
   C. are marsupials
   D. live alone

3. Which information about pandas and koalas is different?
   A. How many different things they eat
   B. How much they can weigh
   C. What their fur protects them from
   D. What they climb

4. Which word or phrase from the passage does NOT signal a comparison?
   A. "but"
   B. "since"
   C. "however"
   D. "in reality"

5. What details from the passage help you know that pandas and koalas are NOT similar animals?

   _____

   _____

   _____

Name _____ Date _____

◀ BUILDING VOCABULARY: Using Context Clues

You will find words as you read that are new to you. Often there will be other words or phrases in the text that will help you determine the meaning of a new word. These other words or phrases are context clues and are usually found in sentences near the new word. Using context clues will help you make logical guesses about the meanings of new words. Locating and using context clues will aid your comprehension and help develop your vocabulary.

Example: They are *solitary* animals, which means they mostly <u>live alone</u>.

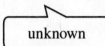 unknown
 context clue

Read each sentence. Look for context clues about the meaning of the word in italics. Underline another word or phrase that helps you understand the word in italics.

1. The panda is likely to be high up in a tree and *apt* to be napping.

2. Most of its food comes from bamboo, which makes it primarily an *herbivore*, or plant-eating animal.

3. The koala is a *marsupial*, like a kangaroo.

4. Koalas are *tree-dwelling* animals, meaning they live only in trees.

5. The koala's diet consists entirely of leaves of *eucalyptus* (yoo ka lip tis), or gum, trees.

6. The zookeeper was *candid*, honestly sharing her opinion on the subject of koalas and pandas.

7. *Nocturnal* animals are only active at night.

8. *Precisely* where was the panda, and exactly what was it doing?

◀ LESSON 5: Identifying Fact and Opinion

Some sentences are **facts**. They have information about something that is known to be true because it has been observed or proven.

Example: Phoenix is the capital of Arizona.

Some sentences are **opinions**. They are about something believed to be true, but which falls short of positive knowledge.

Example: Phoenix is the most beautiful city in the country.

It is important for readers to be able to tell the difference between a fact and an opinion. It helps them know when an author is stating an argument and when he or she is using information to support that argument. Generally, facts are used to support opinions.

Read the paragraph below. Think about whether the ideas in it are facts or opinions.

> Much of Iceland is covered with the sparkling ice of glaciers. They are stunning to see. The third largest glacier in the world is located in Iceland. Only the glaciers in Antarctica and Greenland are bigger. The very thought of their size is amazing. There are so many glaciers in Iceland that they have changed the shape of the land. When a glacier slides down the side of a mountain into the sea, it carves a large channel into the Earth. These channels fill with seawater. The channels are beautiful inlets called fjords. Fjords make up much of the coast of Iceland. The view is marvelous and dramatic.

Name ______________________________ Date ______________

Think about the sentences in the paragraph. Ask yourself whether each of them is about a fact or an opinion. Underline the facts. Circle the opinions. Write three facts and three opinions from the paragraph in the chart below.

Facts	**Opinions**

Name _____ Date _____

Read the passage. Write your answers to the boxed questions as you read to check your understanding.

The Leaning Tower

The Leaning Tower in Pisa, Italy, is located in one of the most beautiful urban squares in the world. Each year, thousands of world travelers visit this unique structure. Without fail, two questions are foremost in the minds of everyone who sees the Leaning Tower—why does it lean and what keeps it wfrom falling over?

---

1. *What is one fact about the location of the Leaning Tower?*

2. *What is one opinion about the location of the Leaning Tower?*

The cause of the tipping is not certain. Some people believe that the lean was intentional—that it was actually planned by the tower's architect. Surveys done in the 1800s, however, probably indicate the real problem. There is a layer of underground water that has weakened the soil beneath the tower.

---

3. *Write two facts about the cause of the tower's lean.*

For years, the tower was stabilized with counterweights. As the years have passed, more and more counterweights have been added to slow the lean, which is currently about one millimeter per year. The tower has been closed to visitors at various times as efforts have been made to find a way to stop the tower from leaning further. So far, these efforts have proven successful. The Leaning Tower of Pisa is one building that is definitely worth saving.

4. *Is the last statement of the passage a fact or an opinion? How do you know?*

5. *What is the most interesting fact about the Leaning Tower of Pisa?*

6. *Is your answer to question 5 a fact or an opinion? Explain.*

◀ **INDEPENDENT PRACTICE: Previewing Vocabulary**

The words in the Word Bank are from the passage you are about to read. Study the definitions.
Complete the activity that follows to get familiar with the words before you begin reading. Write the
correct word in each blank.

Word Bank
tragic — related to a tragedy
spectacular — marvelous
miraculously — in an extraordinary way, as though by a miracle
aloft — up high above the ground
flammable — able to light afire easily and burn
eyewitnesses — people who see something as it happens
pathway — lane or passageway
reminiscent — suggestive, calling to memory

1. The player's _____ accident ended her season.

2. Their performance was _____ of a great rock concert I saw last year.

3. The puppy fell down the side of the mountain and was _____ rescued by
   the hiker.

4. The police officer spoke with all of the _____ to the robbery.

5. The parade floats were stupendous and _____!

6. The rainbow seemed to make a _____ into the clouds.

7. The warning stated that dry trees are very_____.

8. Zooming _____ over the treetops on the zip line was amazing!

Name _____ Date _____

◀ INDEPENDENT PRACTICE: Reading the Passage

Read the passage. As you read, answer the guided reading questions on your own paper.

Incident at Lakehurst

One of the most **tragic** and **spectacular** aviation accidents of all time occurred on the afternoon of May 6, 1937. On that date, the Hindenburg airship, a rigid zeppelin, suddenly burst into flames while attempting to tie onto a mooring tower at the airfield in Lakehurst, New Jersey. Thirty-seven of the Hindenburg's passengers perished in the fiery crash. **Miraculously**, fifty-four people survived.

The 804-foot-long Hindenburg was held **aloft** by 200,000 cubic meters of hydrogen. Hydrogen is an extremely **flammable**, lighter-than-air gas. Originally the Hindenburg, like most zeppelins, had been designed to use helium to fly. Helium is a much more stable, nonflammable gas. Unfortunately, due to the outbreak of World War II in Europe, helium was in short supply. Hydrogen became the most reasonable alternative for these rigid airships.

It is well documented that the Hindenburg was attempting to land in less-than-ideal conditions. The ship had been dodging thunderstorms all afternoon on its final leg from New York City to Lakehurst. The weather forced the Hindenburg to swing far out to sea, which put it behind schedule. Right before the Hindenburg was set to land, a line of strong thunderstorms swept through the Lakehurst area. During the landing, **eyewitnesses** reported seeing flashes of lightning in the distance. There can be no doubt that the weather in and around Lakehurst was very dangerous at the time.

Guided Reading:

1. *What is the author's opinion of the Hindenburg's accident?*

Name _____ Date _____

As usual, the mooring lines were lowered from the ship to waiting attendants on the ground. It is very likely that this connection created a strong ground-to-cloud electrical **pathway**. Just prior to the crash, one observer described a strange blue glow atop the airship. This is called a corona, and it is consistent with strong electrical activity.

Because the Hindenburg burst into flames, most investigators immediately seized upon the obvious explanation: that a hydrogen gas leak was the cause of the crash. But this theory has several holes. First, the Hindenburg did not explode. Hydrogen gas, when ignited, is very explosive. Second, hydrogen produces no visible flame. However, the Hindenburg did catch fire and burn. The fire was very bright and **reminiscent** of what one might see in a forest fire, which was not consistent with burning hydrogen. In addition, not a single eyewitness or survivor reported smelling garlic. The scent of garlic is always added to hydrogen gas so that leaks can be found easily.

Sixty-seven years later, the two remaining samples of the fabric that formed the outer skin of the Hindenburg were tested. One of the samples burned in seconds when exposed to an open flame. The other sample was exposed to an electrical charge. The charge was similar to the kind that would have been present in the air on that stormy evening in 1937. When the charge was run directly through the fabric, it simply burned a hole in it. When the charge was run along the surface of the fabric, as it would have been at Lakehurst, the fabric ignited and disappeared in seconds. These tests showed this fabric to be highly flammable.

Regardless of what caused the Hindenburg disaster, 1937 marked the end of passenger flight on rigid, lighter-than-air ships.

Guided Reading:

2. *Is the statement about what the observer saw a fact or an opinion? How do you know?*

3. *What is one interesting fact about hydrogen?*

◄ **INDEPENDENT PRACTICE: Checking Comprehension**

Circle the best answer for items 1–4. For item 5, write your answer in complete sentences on the lines provided.

1. Which sentence about the passage is an opinion?
   A. The scent of garlic is added to hydrogen.
   B. This theory has several holes.
   C. The airship burst into flames.
   D. The fire was extremely bright.

2. Which fact about the supply of helium in 1937 influenced the Hindenburg disaster?
   A. Helium was very stable.
   B. Helium was not flammable.
   C. There was not much helium.
   D. Airships were designed to use helium.

3. Which description of the Hindenburg accident is an opinion?
   A. It was the most spectacular aviation accident of all time.
   B. The weather around Lakehurst was dangerous at the time.
   C. The Hindenburg caught fire and burned.
   D. The airship burst into flames!

4. One fact about the Hindenburg is that it was —
   A. nonflammable
   B. about 800 feet long
   C. made of pretty fabric
   D. the best airship ever built

5. According to the end of the passage, why does the cause of the Hindenburg disaster remain unknown?

   _____

   _____

   _____

◀ BUILDING VOCABULARY: Using Suffixes

A suffix is a set of letters that can be added to the end of some words. Adding a suffix changes the word's meaning. The suffix -*ly* can be added to the end of nouns and adjectives. The new word formed is an adverb.

-ly	
Meanings	**Examples**
in a certain way	suddenly, easily
like something, or having the character of something	saintly, cowardly
happening at a certain time	daily, yearly

In the selection, the following words all have the suffix -*ly*. Complete each sentence with the correct word.

cowardly   highly   simply

1. She answered the questions _____, without giving extra information.

2. A the sound of thunder, the _____ dog hid under the bed.

3. The whistle is a _____ effective way to stop the game.

Add the suffix -*ly* to each of the words in the box. Use each new word to correctly complete each sentence.

immediate   careful   week

4. Mrs. Watson gets a _____ delivery of groceries every Monday.

5. When I heard the phone ring, I _____ reached to answer it.

6. I _____ moved the glassware out of the cabinet and placed it on the floor.

46

◄ LESSON 6: Identifying Cause and Effect

Many things happen for a reason, so there is a relationship between what happens and why it happens. It's called cause and effect. Authors sometimes write about things that happen and why those things happen. They are writing about causes and effects.

A **cause** is the reason for something. It is an event or a situation that happens or exists first or before something else. An **effect** is what happens as a result of the cause. Of the two related events, it's the one that happens second or last. When you read about events, look for the reason they happen.

Examples: *Andrés became really tired.* **(cause)**
　　　　　　Andrés went to sleep early. **(effect)**

Read the paragraph below. Think about the events and their causes.

> A tornado is a column of air that rotates violently. It extends from within a thundercloud. The funnel cloud must be in contact with both the thundercloud and the ground. Many tornados are formed in a special type of thundercloud. This is known as a supercell. A tornado starts when a current of moist, warm air rises up through the thunderstorm. The result of this activity is damaging. Tornados leave a path of destruction behind them. They have completely destroyed houses. They have flattened entire areas. They can lift up pavement and break it apart. They can also pick up cars and trailers and drop them someplace else. Even objects like sticks have been found driven into trees and brick walls.

Name _____ Date _____

Think about how strong tornados are. In the sample paragraph, how tornadoes form and the damage they cause are described. Underline examples in the paragraph of damage caused by tornadoes. Write three effects of tornadoes in the graphic organizer below.

Cause   **Effect**

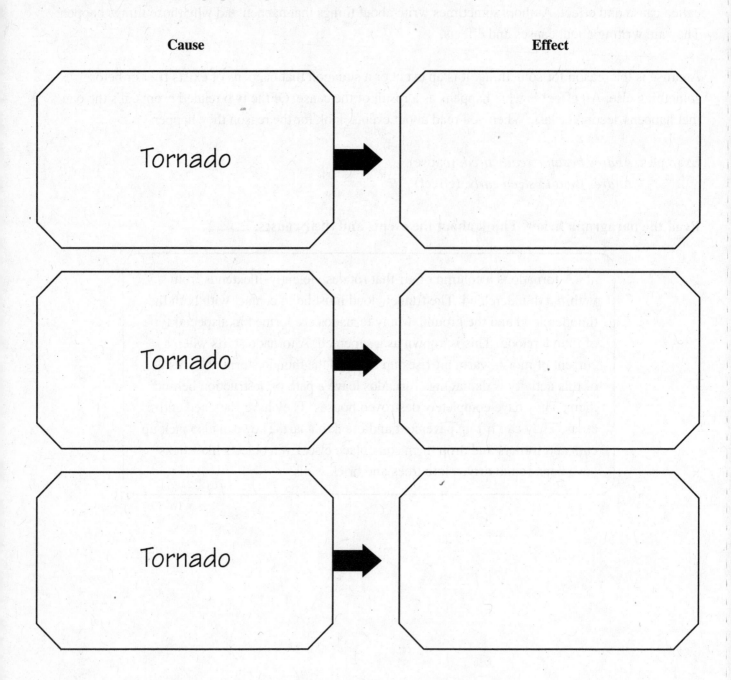

Name _____   Date _____

◀ **GUIDED PRACTICE**

Read the passage. Write your answers to the boxed questions as you read to check your understanding.

Cold Weather Hazards

Winter brings beautiful snowy scenes and fun winter sports. However, cold weather can also bring hazards that can make life difficult or even dangerous. Here are some of these winter hazards.

Snow

When the temperature in a cloud is lower than 32° Fahrenheit, ice crystals begin to form. As the crystals join together and fall, they form snowflakes. Most snowflakes are six-sided, and many look like stars.

---

1. *What causes snowflakes to form?*

If the temperature near the ground is well below freezing, the flakes fall as dry snow. Dry snow is easy for snowplows to scoop and move. But when the temperature is not so cold, the flakes fall as wet snow. Wet snow is heavy and difficult to clear off streets. This kind of snow can make it difficult for people to travel from place to place. It can also pull down power lines.

Any kind of snow can be a problem if there is too much of it. Snowstorms make it difficult to see, causing pedestrians and drivers to become confused and disoriented. They may get lost or have an accident. After the storm, snow can pile up in snowdrifts that cover cars and streets.

---

2. *What effects can snowstorms have on people?*

3. *How do cars and streets become covered in snow?*

Avalanche: Snow on the Move

In the mountains, avalanches are a danger. An avalanche occurs after heaps of snow pile up on a slope. A small movement is sometimes all it takes to start an avalanche. Skiers or hikers often cause avalanches just walking across the snow. First, a small patch of snow starts to slide down a mountain. This causes more snow to slide. The small slide can quickly become a huge wall of snow crashing down the mountain.

---

4. *Sometimes one effect may have several causes. What are two causes of avalanches?*

Dry Avalanche

There are two kinds of avalanches. The most common is a dry avalanche. It is made of dry, powdery snow mixed with air. It can happen anytime there is a new layer of snow. A dry avalanche can travel more than 100 miles per hour! Because it is so light, a dry avalanche is not usually dangerous. But its speed can make it powerful. It can sometimes carry people over cliffs, destroy buildings, and knock down trees.

Name _____ Date _____

◀ INDEPENDENT PRACTICE: Previewing Vocabulary

The words in the Word Bank are from the passage you are about to read. Study the definitions. Complete the activity that follows to get familiar with the words before you begin reading. Write the correct word to complete each sentence.

Word Bank
adverse — bad, damaging
fumes — gas or smoke that is irritating, harmful, or strong
ventilation — the flow or change of air to keep the air fresh
fixed — held steady, securely placed, fastened
christened — given a name or dedicated to

1. Dinner was burning, and thick gray _____ hung in the air.

2. Because the water hose is _____ to the front of the house, the garden hose was not long enough to reach the kitchen.

3. Inside, we all had an _____ reaction to the smell of the burnt meal.

4. Jesse opened the window to provide some _____.

5. Mom _____ the charred pan the Pot of Fire.

◄ INDEPENDENT PRACTICE: Reading the Passage

Read the passage. As you read, answer the guided reading questions on your own paper.

A Tunnel Built

In the early 1900s, the automobile was invented. During the twentieth century, different kinds of vehicles grew in popularity. Many people had a car. The cars allowed people to get around more rapidly.

People in New York City and New Jersey, however, wanted to get back and forth even more quickly. They wanted some way to cross the Hudson River with their vehicles. The Hudson runs between New York City and New Jersey. In 1906, a commission made up of people from these two places was arranged.

The commission wanted to explore the construction of a bridge across the Hudson. That idea was turned down. It would be much too costly. Instead, it was decided that a tunnel beneath the Hudson would be built. One reason for it was that a tunnel would be less affected by **adverse** weather.

The project to build the tunnel was called the "Hudson River Vehicular Tunnel Project." In 1919, Clifford Holland was chosen to lead the project. Construction of the tunnel began in 1920.

The biggest challenge was getting clean air into the tunnel. The fear was that **fumes** from cars would be harmful. These fumes would affect those traveling in the tunnel. So engineers came up with a plan. They built an automatic **ventilation** system. This system would make the air cleaner in the tunnel. It would actually be purer than the air aboveground. This tunnel was the first of its kind. It was the first **fixed** vehicle crossing from New York City to New Jersey. It was also the first mechanically ventilated vehicle tunnel.

Two tunnels were dug: one from New Jersey and one from New York City. The work was difficult. In 1924, tragedy struck the project. Holland passed away. He died one day before the two tunnels were to link up, but construction continued.

Guided Reading:

> 1. *What were the two causes for the decision to build a tunnel instead of a bridge?*

> 2. *What was an effect of the automatic ventilation system?*

Finally, in 1927, the tunnel opened. It was **christened** the
Holland Tunnel after the first chief engineer, Clifford Holland.
The toll for using the tunnel was 50 cents. The ride through the
tunnel was about $1\frac{1}{2}$ miles long. It took drivers about 8 minutes to
pass through.

On the first day of the Holland Tunnel's use, 51,694 vehicles
passed through. Back then, the tunnel cost about $50 million
to build. Today it would cost more than $1.4 billion. The tunnel
is still used in the present day. Since it was built, more than 1.3
billion vehicles have used the tunnel.

Guided Reading:

3. *What was the effect of the death of engineer Clifford Holland?*

◀ INDEPENDENT PRACTICE: Checking Comprehension

Circle the best answer for items 1–4. For item 5, write your answer in complete sentences on the lines provided.

1. Which sentence states one cause for the building of the Holland Tunnel?

   A. The Hudson River runs between New York City and New Jersey.

   B. A commission of people from New York and New Jersey was arranged.

   C. During the twentieth century, different kinds of vehicles grew in popularity.

   D. People in New York City and New Jersey wanted to get back and forth more quickly.

2. What was the cause for worry about fumes in the tunnel?

   A. The engineers had a plan.

   B. The air in the tunnel would be pure.

   C. Fumes would harm people travelling in a tunnel.

   D. A ventilation system would clean fumes out of the air.

3. What was the effect of the worry about fumes in the tunnel?

   A. The tunnel opened in 1927.

   B. People still use the tunnel today.

   C. The tunnel was named after an engineer.

   D. An automatic ventilation system was built.

4. What would be one cause or reason for enlarging the Holland Tunnel?

   A. A lot more traffic will travel between New York and New Jersey.

   B. The cost of the project will be extremely high and unaffordable.

   C. No one knows what to name the new tunnel.

   D. A commission will organize the work.

5. According to the passage, why were people from New York and New Jersey on the commission?

   _____

   _____

   _____

Name _____   Date _____

◀ BUILDING VOCABULARY: Using Root Words

A root word is the simplest form of a word. A root word can be used as a base for making other words. Suffixes and prefixes are added to root words. Suffixes and prefixes change the meaning of the root word.

Below are some common prefixes and suffixes and their meanings.

Prefix	Meaning	Suffix	Meaning
dis-	lack of, not, away	*-ity*	state or quality
auto-	self	*-ly, -ily*	manner

In the passage, the following root words all have the suffix -*ly*. Write the correct word to complete each sentence.

actual	cost	final	quick

1. Construction of the new school was _____ but the students were pleased.

2. After an hour, she _____ crossed the finish line.

3. He knew his math facts well, so he answered the questions _____.

4. The ad said $5, but the doll did _____ cost $6.

The following words both contain the root word *mob*, which means "move." Write the correct word to complete each sentence.

mobility	automobile

5. An _____ is a self-propelled vehicle with a motor and four wheels.

6. Her _____ was greatly affected when she had foot surgery.

◄ LESSON 7: Recognizing Author's Purpose

Author's purpose is the reason why an author has written a text for readers. Authors write to inform, to entertain, or to persuade readers. To inform, authors may give you facts or true information about a subject. When authors entertain, they tell a story or describe real or imaginary characters, places, and events. Authors who write to persuade want readers to agree with their opinion. Authors may provide facts or opinions to support their opinion.

It is important to recognize the author's purpose for writing what you are reading. Knowing the author's purpose helps prepare you for the type of information you will read. You can adjust your reading method to match the author's purpose in order to better understand and remember what you are reading.

Read the paragraph below. Think about the author's purpose for writing.

> I don't know about you, but I hate trash and filth. Unfortunately, that is what we have been living next to for years. Rotary Park is in bad condition. The trash cans are overflowing. The grass is covered in garbage. The walls and buildings are covered with graffiti—most of which is not appropriate for our children. The playground is falling apart and is dangerous for our kids. Our community needs to pull together and restore the park to its original beauty. First, we need to write the city leaders to demand that they clean it up. If that does not work, we need to take the lead. We will clean it up ourselves! We could organize several Saturday cleanup days. With the motivated people in this community, we will be able to reclaim our beautiful park.

1. What is the author's message?

   _____

   _____

2. What do you think is the author's purpose for writing?

   _____

   _____

◀ **GUIDED PRACTICE**

Read the passage. Write your answers to the boxed questions as you read to check your understanding.

A Delicious Mistake

Most of us eat bread on a daily basis. Have you ever wondered who invented bread? The legend of how bread was first made goes back to ancient Egypt, around the year 2600 BC.

1. *What do you think the author is going to write about?*

An Egyptian slave was baking flour-and-water cakes. That evening, he fell asleep while the cakes were baking, and the fire went out. During the night, the dough fermented and puffed up. The flour, liquid, and honey that were in the dough had probably been exposed to some sort of wild yeast or floating bacteria. Because the dough was kept warm, the yeast (or bacteria) cells grew, causing the dough to rise.

When the slave awoke, the dough was twice its size. He simply pushed it back into the oven to cook. He did not want anyone to find out that he had fallen asleep while baking the bread.

2. *Why do you think the author is writing this as a story?*

The slave's master discovered the mistake but did not punish the man for falling asleep. Instead, the master discovered that the new cake was delicious. The ancient Egyptians continued to bake using yeast. Their civilization produced the world's finest bakers.

3. *What do you think the author's purpose for writing the passage was? Explain your answer.*

Name _____ Date _____

The words in the Word Bank are from the passage you are about to read. Study the definitions. Complete the activity that follows to get familiar with the words before you begin reading. Write each answer on the lines provided.

Word Bank

seasoned — experienced

novices — people with little or no experience

equestrians — people who ride on horseback

introductory — providing someone with a beginning knowledge or first experience of something

fearless — without fear

---

1. *Equus* is a Latin word for "horse." How is the word *equus* related to *equestrians*?

_____

2. How are the words *fear* and *fearless* related?

_____

3. How do you think the words *introduce* and *introductory* are related?

_____

_____

4. *Novus* means "new" in Latin. How are the words *novice* and *novus* related?

_____

_____

5. One meaning of *season* is "to fully develop." Explain what *seasoned* means.

_____

_____

Name _____ Date _____

◀ **INDEPENDENT PRACTICE:** Reading the Passage

Read the passage. As you read, answer the guided reading questions on your own paper.

Horsing Around Riding Center

Do you love horses?

Have you always wanted to
learn to ride horseback?

Come to Horsing Around Riding Center!

We make horseback riding fun!

No matter who you are, Horsing Around Riding Center is the place for you:

• All ages are welcome!   • **Seasoned** riders can *improve*.

• **Novices** can *learn* to ride.   • Have fun at *every* lesson

Horseback riders always have fun at Horsing Around Riding Center! It doesn't matter whether you have never ridden a horse before. We have classes for beginners and experienced **equestrians**.

We offer the following classes for beginning riders:

Age	Class
6 to 8	Peanuts on Ponies
8 to 12	Kids Can Ride
12 to 18	Terrific Teens
Over 18	Adult Adventures

Contact Us!
Horsing Around Riding Center
15 Morgan Lane
Holbrook, New Hampshire 33950
(634) 667-4435
Visit us online!

Guided Reading:

1. *What do you think this passage is about?*

2. *How is the author presenting the information? Why?*

Name _____ Date _____

Customers' Comments

"I was afraid to ride at first, but I relaxed during my **introductory** lesson. And I had fun! Soon, I was **fearless**. I enjoyed every lesson after that, too. This is the best place to learn to ride!"

— *Maya Jonas, age 12*

"The class for teens is outstanding! My friends and I had never been near a horse before we joined the Terrific Teens class. Now we ride every week during our summer vacation."

— *Oscar, age 17*

Guided Reading:

3. *Why do you think the author included two people's experiences in the ad?*

4. *Why do you think the author wrote this passage?*

Recognizing Author's Purpose
Reading Intervention, Grade 6

◄ INDEPENDENT PRACTICE: Checking Comprehension

Circle the best answer for items 1–4. For item 5, write your answer in complete sentences on the lines provided.

1. The author asks questions at the top of the ad in order to —
   A. make readers interested
   B. share the success of one young rider
   C. tell where the riding center is located.
   D. give readers information about classes

2. Which of these sentences is a stated fact in the ad?
   A. "We make horseback riding fun!"
   B. "The class for teens is outstanding!"
   C. "This is the best place to learn to ride!"
   D. "We have classes for beginners and experienced equestrians."

3. The author includes ages with the class chart for beginners to inform readers that —
   A. there are only classes for beginners
   B. there are classes for young children
   C. beginners can be people of any age
   D. beginners will have fun

4. The author writes this passage in order to —
   A. educate readers about the horses at Horsing Around Riding Center
   B. explain how riding at Horsing Around Riding Center is good exercise
   C. encourage people to take riding classes at Horsing Around Riding Center
   D. tell readers to visit at Horsing Around Riding Center and other riding centers

5. Does the passage convince you to take horseback riding lessons at Horsing Around Riding Center? List two reasons why the passage made you more or less excited to take riding lessons.

   _____

   _____

   _____

◀ BUILDING VOCABULARY: Using Synonyms

Remember that synonyms are words that have the same or nearly the same meaning. For example, in the sentence below, the words *label* and *tag* are synonyms.

> The label on the shirt said SMALL, but the tag with the price said MEDIUM.

Authors use synonyms in their writing to avoid repeating a word or words. Synonyms help to make the text more interesting. Readers can use synonyms to determine the meaning of unfamiliar words and to better understand what they read.

Decide which vocabulary word means the same or almost the same as the underlined word or phrase. Write the correct vocabulary word on the line.

equestrians	introductory	seasoned
fearless	novices	

1. He looked everyone in the eye as though he were <u>unafraid</u>.

   _____

2. Three <u>experienced</u> astronauts landed on the Moon.

   _____

3. I was amazed by how healthy <u>horseback riders</u> are.

   _____

4. The band of <u>beginners</u> played the songs well.

   _____

5. The <u>opening</u> speech put everyone at ease.

   _____

Name _____   Date _____

◄ LESSON 8: Making Inferences

Sometimes when you read, you have to figure out what the author means. An **inference** is an educated guess based on information. Generalizations, predictions, and conclusions are all types of inferences.

To make inferences, readers connect information stated in the text and information that is <u>not</u> stated, such as what they already know from their own knowledge and experience. We can check that our inferences are reasonable by finding words, phrases, sentences, and prior experiences or knowledge that support the conclusion.

Read the paragraph below. Think about making inferences while you read.

> Every child should learn to play a musical instrument and to appreciate music. Music is an important part of cultures all over the world. It brings beauty and harmony into people's lives. It also makes us use our brain in a different way. That is why I think that we need more music programs and lessons in all schools.

1. What inference can you make about the author of this paragraph? Write this in the circle below.

2. What details from the paragraph provides evidence for this inference? Write the details in the ovals below.

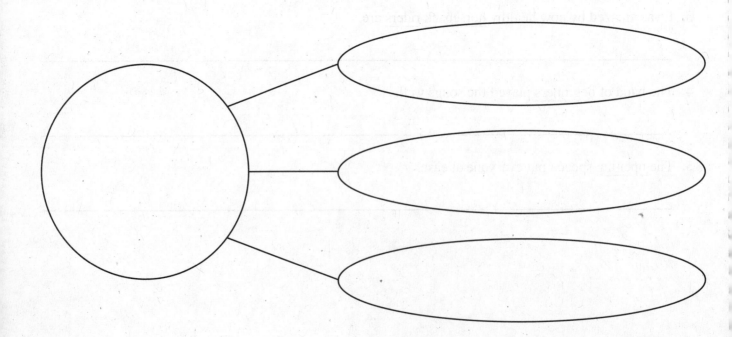

Name _____ Date _____

◀ GUIDED PRACTICE

Read the passage. Write your answers to the boxed questions as you read to check your understanding.

Growing Giant Sunflowers

Some Really Big Flowers

The size, height, and beauty of giant sunflowers attract many gardeners. Normally, giant sunflowers grow to be about 7 to 10 feet tall. Their flowers grow to be about 12 inches across. That's bigger than a basketball! Some people, though, try to grow their flowers even larger. In 1983, a woman in Canada grew a sunflower that was more than 32 inches across. That's as wide as an open umbrella! Then in 1986, a person in the Netherlands grew a sunflower that was more than 25 feet tall. That's taller than many people's houses! These flowers both set world records. Growing sunflowers of your own can be a lot of fun, whether you set records or not.

Getting Started

Giant sunflowers are perfect for young gardeners. The seeds are large and easy to sow when the soil is loose. Plants shoot up quickly in hot weather and grow well in almost any type of soil. The amount of sunshine your flowers get will affect how they grow. For larger flowers, the side of a building or a fence facing south is a perfect place for planting. If you would like your plants to be very tall, try planting on the side facing north. The plants will grow taller from having to stretch to reach the morning sun.

> **1.** *What inference does the author make in this paragraph about young gardeners?*

Caring for Your Sunflowers

Once your baby plants start to sprout up out of the soil, water them just once a week. Give them a heavy soaking of water. That way the water will go deeper into the ground. Then the new roots will have to grow farther into the earth to get the water. This makes the roots stronger. Strong roots are needed to hold up the tall, heavy sunflowers. Once your sunflowers grow bigger, start giving them less water more often. A light watering once every evening can work very well.

2. *What inference can you make about water?*

3. *What do you already know about growing sunflowers?*

Did you know that plants need vitamins just like people do? The people who grow the biggest sunflowers use fertilizer in the soil. Different types of fertilizers help the sunflowers grow in different ways. Some fertilizers make them taller; others make them larger or healthier. You can find out more about fertilizers at a local garden store.

Planting Directions

 Step 1

Choose a location that gets lots of sunshine.

 Step 2

Wait until the last danger of frost is past before planting.

 Step 3

Turn the soil until it is loose.

 Step 4

Plant seeds about 1 inch deep.

Step 5

Pack soil firmly over seeds with your hand.

 Step 6

Spray water gently over the seeds.

 Step 7

Keep the soil extra moist for 3 to 7 days.

Not Just for Show

   One of the best things about sunflowers is their delicious seeds. To save your giant sunflower seeds, cover each flower head with a paper bag. Do this as soon as the flowers begin to dry out. As the seeds ripen, this will protect them from hungry birds. You can roast your sunflower seeds in the oven or eat them straight off the dried flowers. Don't forget to save some seeds for next year's garden!

4. *What inference can you make about whether the author grows sunflowers?*

5. *Why do you feel your inference is reasonable?*

◀ INDEPENDENT PRACTICE: Previewing Vocabulary

The words in the Word Bank are from the passage you are about to read. Study the definitions. Complete the activity that follows to get familiar with the words before you begin reading. Write the correct word to complete each sentence.

Word Bank

pursue — to follow in order to catch

revelation — something that is made known or realized, especially something surprising

baiting — trying to anger someone by teasing or nagging

contemplating — thinking seriously about something

sprinted — moved rapidly or at top speed for a brief period

---

1. My dog would love to _____ the neighbor's cat, but we keep him on a leash.

2. The runners _____ to the finish line.

3. When Jon simply ignored his little sister's teasing, she gave up _____ him.

4. Jen was _____ bidding on the bright painting when Tony announced the silent auction was closed.

5. The _____ that the prize was a new car thrilled the game show winner.

Name _____ Date _____

Read the passage. As you read, answer the guided reading questions on your own paper.

Why the Crocodile Has a Bumpy Back:
A Folktale from Angola

Long ago, the crocodile's back was as smooth and soft as a little child's back. One afternoon, the crocodile was taking a nap beside the river. Unexpectedly, the rabbit came dashing along and bumped right into him.

"Rabbit," said the crocodile, "why did you wake me? And why are you all out of breath?"

"I have been running away from the dog all morning," the rabbit panted. "A man sent him to **pursue** me. I think the man wants to have me for his dinner!" Suddenly, the rabbit had a **revelation** that made him nervous. "*You're* not hungry, are you, Crocodile?" he asked uneasily.

"No," said the lazy crocodile. "I've already had my dinner. It was unbelievably delicious."

The rabbit gave a sigh of relief. "That's good," he said. "I've had enough trouble for one day."

"Well," said the crocodile, "I never have any trouble. In fact, I bet Trouble would be afraid to bother me."

"I don't think you should talk like that," the rabbit warned him. "Trouble might not like to hear you to talk about him that way. You're only **baiting** Trouble to show you his bad side. "

The rabbit hopped off, anxious again to get further away from the dog.

The crocodile, though, could not stop **contemplating** what Rabbit had said. The more he thought, the more angry he became. At last, he decided to go find Trouble and tell him to mind his own business.

Guided Reading:

1. *What inference can you make about what makes Rabbit nervous?*

As he trampled through the bushes, the crocodile frightened the flamingo, who was standing in the river. Startled, the flamingo flapped up into the air, which startled the monkey, who had just lit the candles on his birthday cake. The monkey shrieked and bounded away to hide, knocking over the birthday cake. The candle flames set fire to the tall, dry grass.

As the flames grew higher and higher around the crocodile, he **sprinted** toward the river. The flames licked at his back and scorched his soft skin. By the time he reached the safety of the cool water, his back was burned and rough. Ever since then, the crocodile's back has been bumpy, and he's been an unhappy, grumpy fellow.

Guided Reading:

2. *What inference can you make about what the crocodile will do the next time he hears about Trouble?*

◀ INDEPENDENT PRACTICE: Checking Comprehension

Circle the best answer for items 1–4. For item 5, write your answer in complete sentences on the lines provided.

1. Why doesn't the crocodile eat the rabbit?
   A. He has already eaten.
   B. He thinks rabbits taste bad.
   C. He is afraid of Trouble.
   D. Rabbits have too much fur.

2. Why does the crocodile have a bumpy back?
   A. The crocodile was born with a bumpy back.
   B. His back was badly burned, and it became rough and bumpy.
   C. He stayed underwater for so long that his back became bumpy.
   D. The rabbit chased him into a fire.

3. The monkey probably usually responds to being startled by—
   A. hiding away and crying
   B. laughing and turning away
   C. climbing higher into the trees
   D. running wildly and thrashing about

4. What helps you infer that this passage is a fable?
   A. It involves talking animal characters.
   B. It contains a lot of facts that can be proven.
   C. It is meant to persuade.
   D. It is a true story.

5. What inference can you make about what Rabbit might say the next time he sees Crocodile? Why?

   _____

   _____

   _____

   _____

◀ BUILDING VOCABULARY: Using Root Words

A root word is the simplest form of a word that can be used as a base for making other words. Suffixes and prefixes are added to root words. Adding suffixes and prefixes changes the meaning of the root word.

These are examples of prefixes and suffixes and their meaning.

Prefix	Meaning	Suffix	Meaning
un-	not, reverse of	*-ness*	noun, state, condition, quality
mal-	bad	*-ily, -ly*	manner

Happy is a commonly used root word. Write the meaning of each new word and use the new word in a sentence.

1. unhappy _____

_____

2. happily _____

_____

3. unhappily _____

_____

4. happiness _____

_____

The following words both contain the root word easy. Write the correct word to complete each sentence.

uneasy   easily

5. Rabbit would have felt _____ around Crocodile if Crocodile were hungry.

6. Monkey _____ blew out all the candles on the cake with little effort.

◀ LESSON 9: Drawing Conclusions

When you **draw a conclusion**, you make a judgment based on information you already know. You do this often in everyday life. For example, the car in front of you in traffic has license plates from another state. So you conclude, or draw the conclusion, that the owners have moved to your town from another state.

You can also use the skill of drawing conclusions after you have finished reading something. To draw a conclusion, you form an opinion or evaluation about a text based on information the author has both stated and implied. You also base your conclusion on your own experiences and on other things you have read. By drawing conclusions, you demonstrate your ability to grasp the important ideas of the text. You can use this skill for both fiction and nonfiction writing.

For any conclusion you draw, ask yourself if it makes sense. Also, you should be able to support your conclusion. To do this, use evidence from the text. (Note that the evidence may be more involved than one or two sentences directly taken from the text.) Also use supporting ideas from your own life experiences.

Read the paragraph below. As you read, look for evidence that will allow you to draw a conclusion from the information.

> Coral polyps come in different colors and hundreds of species. Brain coral has tight folds that look like a brain. Divers must be careful not to touch fire coral. It stings! Some corals are called soft coral because their skeletons are less rigid. Lettuce coral look like. . .well, you guess.

1. What conclusion can you draw about coral?

_____

_____

2. Underline the sentences in the paragraph that provide support for this conclusion.

_____

_____

Name _____ Date _____

Read the passage. Write your answers to the boxed questions as you read to check your understanding.

Contact Lenses

Contact lenses are thin discs that lie on the surface of your eye. In reality, they rest on the cornea, which is the clear covering of your eye. The cornea protects the pupil and the colored part of your eye, called the iris. Contact lenses help correct your vision. They work just like an ordinary pair of glasses.

Today, contact lenses are made of a very soft material—usually pliable plastic. This material rarely causes discomfort and is very strong. Some lenses are daily wear, which means that they are worn only one day, and then they are cleaned to be worn again. Other contacts are disposable. They are worn for several weeks and then thrown out. If you wear contacts too long, your eyes may begin to get dry. The contacts may also become dirty. These problems make the contact lenses uncomfortable for the wearer.

For some people, it is difficult to get used to wearing contact lenses. Others have trouble placing their finger near or on their eye to insert contact lenses. But if you weigh the options, it is much more convenient to wear contact lenses than to wear glasses.

---

1. *What conclusion about contact lenses can you draw after reading the passage?*

2. *What evidence in the passage supports your conclusion?*

Name _____ Date _____

◀ INDEPENDENT PRACTICE: Previewing Vocabulary

The words in the Word Bank are from the passage you are about to read. Study the definitions. Complete the activity that follows to get familiar with the words before you begin reading. Write the correct word to complete each sentence.

Word Bank
inhibited — unlikely to take action
nutritious — containing a lot of nutrients like vitamins and minerals
heroism — courage and behavior like that of a hero
organization — group of people working together toward a particular purpose
headed — directed, was leader of

1. No longer _____, the young man in college marched in protests and spoke at rallies.

2. Gina made sure her family ate healthy, _____ meals.

3. The young soldier was honored for her _____ in saving the lives of many in her battalion.

4. The _____ I belong to provides support for single parents raising children.

5. The minister _____ the committee for several years.

◄ **INDEPENDENT PRACTICE: Reading the Passage**

Read the passage. As you read, answer the guided reading questions on your own paper.

Unstoppable Clara Barton

Clara Barton was born in 1821 in Massachusetts. She was always a bright and independent child, though somewhat **inhibited**. As she grew older, she discovered that she enjoyed nursing the sick and helping people in need.

The Civil War

In 1861, when the Civil War broke out, Clara Barton went to work helping wounded soldiers. She had to make **nutritious** food from limited supplies, comfort the patients, make sure they had water, and assist the surgeons in dangerous battlefield conditions. Clara did it all, and she did it well.

After the Civil War ended, Clara Barton gave public talks about her experiences. This was a time before movies, radio, or television. One form of entertainment was to go to a public hall to hear someone speak about interesting events. Clara's talks were popular. Before long, her **heroism** and hard work on the battlefields became known throughout the country.

The Red Cross

In 1869, Clara Barton visited Switzerland. She learned about the Red Cross, an **organization** that helped people in times of war and disaster. She decided to start an branch in the United States. Due to her efforts, the American Red Cross became a reality in 1881.

Clara Barton **headed** the American Red Cross until she was 82. Monuments honoring her war work and her life of service can be seen at Antietam National Battlefield and at her final home in Glen Echo, Maryland.

Guided Reading:

1. *What conclusion can you draw relating Clara Burton's work during the Civil War to her personality?*

2. *What conclusion can you draw about the Red Cross in Switzerland?*

◀ **INDEPENDENT PRACTICE: Checking Comprehension**

Circle the best answer for items 1–4. For item 5, write your answer in complete sentences on the lines provided.

1. From the information in the passage, you can draw the conclusion that Clara Barton —
   A. did not like to travel
   B. was sorry for many of her actions
   C. was deeply affected by her experiences during the Civil War
   D. enjoyed public speaking more than she enjoyed helping others

2. What happened because of Clara Barton's visit to Switzerland?
   A. People built monuments to honor Clara Barton.
   B. She started a branch in the United States of the Red Cross.
   C. She decided to give public talks about her experiences.
   D. Clara Barton became famous for her work during the Civil War.

3. What conclusion can you draw about Clara Burton's feelings about soldiers?
   A. Their cause was important and honest.
   B. She was eager to ease their suffering.
   C. She was angry about their involvement in the war.
   D. They needed all the food and supplies she could get.

4. What evidence from the passage supports the conclusion drawn in item 3?
   A. Clara Barton has been honored with several monuments.
   B. Clara Barton traveled after the war.
   C. Clara Barton gave talks about the war.
   D. Clara Barton worked hard to care for soldiers.

5. What conclusion can you draw about why Clara Burton is called *unstoppable*?

   _____

   _____

   _____

   _____

Name _____ Date _____

◂ BUILDING VOCABULARY: Using Prefixes

A prefix is a set of letters that can be added to the beginning of some words. Adding a prefix changes the word's meaning. The prefixes *in-* and *un-* both mean "not."

	Meanings	**Examples**
un-	not	unfriendly
in-	not	invisible

In the passage, the following words have the prefixes *in-* and *un-*. Write the correct word to complete each sentence.

independent   unstoppable

1. The forest fire seemed _____, but we put it out in an hour.

2. She was an extremely _____ individual, so she did not ask for help.

Add the prefix *in-* or *un-* to each word in the box. Write a new word to complete each sentence.

able	active	sane
ravel	covered	credible

3. The old television set stood _____ and forgotten in a corner.

4. They _____ the cake and shouted, 'Surprise!"

5. I was _____ to lift the heavy boxes, so I left them where they were.

6. People thought we were _____ for running barefoot through the snow in the freezing weather.

7. Superman gets dressed with _____ speed.

8. The threads of yarn were not easy to _____ because they were so tangled.

◀ LESSON 10: Summarizing

To **summarize** a passage is to rewrite the important information of a passage in your own words. The important information that a reader should summarize is what a story or text is mostly about, who the people or characters are and what they do, and what events happen.

It is important to be able to summarize a passage in order to better remember what was read, to tell others about the information contained in the passage, and to arrange the ideas in a way that is easy to understand.

Read the paragraphs below. As you read, think about how the text can best be summarized.

> Hansen Gregory was born in 1832 in Camden, Maine, and died in 1921. He is buried in the Sailors' Snug Harbor Cemetery in Germantown, Maine. During the eighty-nine years that Hanson Gregory lived, he spent many of them as a sea captain. A legend says that is where he invented the doughnut hole.
>
> One night, Captain Gregory was eating a fried cake when a violent storm suddenly arose. The captain needed both hands to steer the ship so he shoved the cake over one of the spokes of the ship's helm. Without thinking, he had invented the doughnut hole.

1. What is the main idea of these paragraphs?

_____

_____

2. Name three important words or phrases that should be included in the summary of the paragraphs.

_____

_____

3. Write a summary of the paragraphs.

_____

_____

_____

_____

◀ GUIDED PRACTICE

Read the passage. Write your answers to the boxed questions as you read to check your understanding.

Jump Right In!
adapted from the Aesop's fable "The Fisherman and the Tunny-fish"

The fishermen of Baytown were very worried and frustrated at the same time. They had been going out every day to fish but had caught nothing for several weeks. They all sat in their boats with their poles in the water. No fish were even nibbling on their lines. The fishermen all sat there feeling very dejected and sad. They sat there day after day, but still they came home with nothing.

> **1.** *What details from this paragraph should you include in a summary?*

One day while the fishermen were trying their luck once again, it began raining. The rain came down in droves, causing the fishermen to begin rowing back to shore.

> **2.** *Should you include details from this paragraph in a summary? Explain your answer.*

Under the water, the fish were very excited. They had not come up from the bottom of the bay for days because the weather above was dry and hot. This made the shallow water very warm and uncomfortable for the fish. However, the cool rain lured them to the top. The fish were so thrilled about the rain that they began jumping out of the water.

> **3.** *Should a summary of this passage include the idea, found in the paragraph above, that the shallow water was very warm and uncomfortable for the fish? Why or why not?*

This was a mistake, since all the fishermen were heading toward shore. The fish, with thumps and bumps, began landing in the fishermen's boats. The fishermen were overjoyed at their dumb luck. Now the fishermen had plenty of fish to feed their families. They also had enough to sell at the market.

4. *Write a summary of the passage.*

◀ INDEPENDENT PRACTICE: Previewing Vocabulary

The words in the Word Bank are from the passage you are about to read. Study the definitions. Complete the activity that follows to get familiar with the words before you begin reading. Write the correct word that completes each sentence.

Word Bank
monarch — a ruler such as a king or queen
betrothed — promised to give in marriage; promised to marry
departed — left, went away
eldest — born first, oldest
perceive — to become aware of something though the senses, such as sight
gleaming — shining, glowing

1. Queen Victoria was the first _____ he met.

2. We waved goodbye, got into the car, and _____ for the museum.

3. As the clouds parted, my family was able to _____ the magnificent Grand Canyon before us.

4. In the play, a couple was _____ before they ever met, and the error of their parents' matchmaking had to be fixed before they married.

5. The gem displayed in the window was _____ all day long.

6. My father's _____ brother is my grandmother's first son.

◀ INDEPENDENT PRACTICE: Reading the Passage

Read the passage. As you read, answer the guided reading questions on your own paper.

Which Shall She Choose?
adapted from an Asian folktale

There once lived a king who had three sons like three perfect gems. The three princes were in love with a beautiful princess from a nearby kingdom. The **monarch** told his sons, "Whoever brings me the most precious object will be **betrothed** to the princess."

So the king's three sons **departed** the kingdom in search of the most precious object. They traveled in different directions and promised to meet again in one year.

The **eldest** son was tall and strong. He traveled to an icy northern city. There, he met a merchant selling a small carpet for forty bags of gold. "Why does this rug cost so much?" he asked.

"This is a magic rug," replied the merchant. "When you sit on it and tell it where to go, it will transport you to that place instantly."

To test the carpet's magic, the eldest son wished himself to the other side of town. As in a flash, he was there, so he returned to the merchant and paid forty bags of gold for the magic rug.

The king's second-born son was weaker than his brother, so he traveled to a warmer city far to the south. There, he met a merchant selling a simple wooden tube straight as a rod. He was selling this object for fifty bags of gold. "Why does this wooden tube cost so much?" asked the second son.

"This is a magic tube," replied the merchant. "When you look through this tube, you see any place in the world you wish to **perceive**."

The second son held the tube up to his eye and wished to see his father. Instantly, he saw the king sitting on his throne, awaiting the return of his sons. The king's second son paid the merchant fifty bags of gold for the magic tube.

The king's youngest son journeyed west over many mountains and across great deserts. Finally, he came to a beautiful city along the wide, blue sea. In this city, he met a merchant selling a **gleaming** glass apple that flashed in the sunlight like a diamond. It was not real, but the merchant was selling it for sixty bags of gold.

Guided Reading:

> 1. *Who are the main characters in this passage?*

Summarizing
Reading Intervention, Grade 6

"Why does this glass apple cost so much?" the king's youngest son asked.

"This apple can cure the sick no matter how ill they are," replied the merchant.

Just as the merchant was finishing his reply, a stranger walked by and said, "My wife is deathly ill. Let us test the apple on her." The merchant agreed, and all three men went to the stranger's house. The merchant held the apple before the woman, and in a few moments she was cured. After seeing this, the youngest son bought the healing apple.

A year had passed by the time the three brothers met on a road about two hundred miles away from their father's kingdom. Each son showed the magic of the precious object he had purchased. When the middle son looked through the magic tube, he saw the princess lying in her bed, sick and dying.

"My brothers!" he exclaimed, "The princess is dying! How can we save her life?"

The youngest brother said, "I can use my healing apple to restore her health, but we must get there quickly."

The oldest brother said, "We can use the magic rug to get there immediately."

So all three brothers jumped onto the magic rug, and instantly they were in front of the princess's bed. The youngest son held the healing apple in front of the princess's nose, and in no time she was well again. But who was to marry her?

All the objects were precious, and each had a special gift, so the king with three sons and the king with the princess left the decision up to her.

And she chose the youngest son. For she had loved him all along, and it was his healing apple that saved her life.

Guided Reading:

2. *What main events have happened in this story so far?*

3. *Would you include details of the sons' conversation in your summary? Why or why not?*

4. *Write a summary of the passage.*

◀ INDEPENDENT PRACTICE: Checking Comprehension

Circle the best answer for items 1–4. For item 5, write your answer in complete sentences on the lines provided.

1. The information about the king that should be in a summary is that he—
   A. has a neighboring kingdom
   B. knows a princess
   C. has three sons
   D. is a monarch

2. What important thing do the king's sons do?
   A. They leave the king behind.
   B. They use their precious objects.
   C. They talk with merchants.
   D. They travel to different regions.

3. What event in the passage is needed for a summary?
   A. Where each son traveled
   B. Which son was the strongest
   C. Saving the stranger's wife
   D. Saving the princess

4. Which character is <u>not</u> needed in a summary of the passage?
   A. The stranger
   B. The princess
   C. The second son
   D. The eldest son

5. Write a summary of the passage. Use three pieces of information.

   _____

   _____

   _____

   _____

Name _____ Date _____

◀ BUILDING VOCABULARY: Understanding Figurative Language

Writers often use figurative language, or figures of speech, to help their readers visualize or imagine the images they are describing. Read about one type of figure of speech below.

A simile is a comparison between two unlike things. In a simile, the author uses *like*, *as*, or *as if* to make a comparison. To identify a simile in a passage, look for comparisons. Check whether the comparison is made using *like*, *as*, or *as if*.

Simile: compares two unlike things using "like," "as," or "as if"
Examples: Stacy's hair was like straw. Her smile was as bright as a star. Nicolás ran as if he were a rushing stream.

Read the following sentences. Decide whether or not they contain similes. Put an X in the correct column.

Sentence	Simile?	
	Yes	No
1. This king had three sons like three gems.		
2. One of the sons traveled to a warmer city far to the south.		
3. The youngest son was weaker than his brother.		
4. The simple wooden tube was as straight as a rod.		
5. The sons traveled to the princess with great speed.		
6. The glass apple flashed in the sunlight like a diamond.		
7. The magic rug was as soft as cotton.		
8. The younger son really liked the end of the passage.		

Name _____   Date _____

◀ LESSON 11: Understanding Plot

The **plot** is what happens in a story. The events of a story usually revolve around some problem or struggle. At the end of the story, the problem is usually solved.

Authors use characters to develop plots. A character's actions determine the sequence of story events that make up the plot. The reasons for a character's actions are motives. A motive explains why a character does a specific thing.

Read the paragraph below. As you read, think about the elements of the plot.

> On the day of his first bike race, Kent was nervous, but he knew he was ready. He rode his bike to the starting line with the rest of the riders. He tightened his helmet and steadied himself on his bike. The announcer yelled, "Go!" and the riders were off. Kent soon found himself right behind the lead rider. Soon, there was one lap to go, and Kent pushed himself even though he was tired. He found himself gaining speed and passing the lead rider. He crossed the finish line first and won the bike race!

Name _____ Date _____

Fill in the chart below to tell about the paragraph you just read.

How this story started:

What happened next:

How the problem is solved:

What I think the problem is:

Name _____ Date _____

Read the passage. Write your answers to the boxed questions as you read to check your understanding.

The Forgotten Ear of Corn
adapted from a Native American tale

A Native American woman was collecting corn one day. She wanted to have plenty of corn to last throughout the winter. She went from cornstalk to cornstalk, carefully tore off the ears of corn, and placed them in her basket. When her basket was overflowing, the woman started to leave.

---

1. *What does the woman do at the beginning of the passage?*

As she was walking away, she heard a tiny voice crying, "Please take me with you!" The woman was startled, for she couldn't believe that a child was lost in the cornfield. The woman put down her basket and returned to look for the child, but she could find nothing. So the woman started to leave again.

But again, she heard the tiny voice crying, "Please take me with you!" Again, the woman returned to the cornfield to search for the child.

---

2. *What is the problem in the passage?*

Finally, in one corner of the field, the woman found a tiny ear of corn that was hidden by the leaves of the stalks. The woman knew at once that this tiny ear of corn had been crying out to her. The woman tore off the tiny ear of corn and placed it in her basket with the rest of the corn she had collected. Ever since, Native American women have carefully gathered their corn so that no ear is forgotten or wasted.

---

3. *How is the problem solved?*

◄ INDEPENDENT PRACTICE: Previewing Vocabulary

The words in the Word Bank are from the passage you are about to read. Study the definitions. Complete the activity that follows to get familiar with the words before you begin reading. Write the letter of the correct word to complete each sentence.

Word Bank
acquire — get; come to have
vendors — sellers; merchants
handcrafted — made and decorated by hand
mistreated — treated badly
insane — crazy; mad

1. The excited children ran around laughing and screaming as though they were _____.

   a. acquire   **b.** insane

2. The outdoor market has several jewelry _____ to choose from.

   a. vendors   **b.** handcrafted

3. She wanted to _____ an antique car but didn't have enough money.

   a. insane   **b.** acquire

4. He decided to adopt the puppy that had been _____ and give it a good home.

   a. handcrafted   **b.** mistreated

5. The _____ wardrobe was beautifully made.

   a. mistreated   **b.** handcrafted

Name _____   Date _____

◀ INDEPENDENT PRACTICE: Reading the Passage

Read the passage. As you read, answer the guided reading questions on your own paper.

Riding a Donkey to Learn About the World
adapted from a Nigerian folktale

There once lived a man named Tunde, who lived in the bush country of Nigeria in a palm-roofed house. Tunde wanted to learn more about the world outside his village. He was very restless and wanted to leave his village to **acquire** more knowledge.

One day, Tunde announced to the people of his village that he and his son, Usman, must go on a long journey to learn more about the world. He said, "We have much to learn that cannot be discovered in our tiny village."

Early the next morning, Tunde and Usman packed plenty of food and water onto their donkey and set out on their journey.

After traveling many days through the dry African bush lands and through a beautiful rain forest, they came to a large village. In the village was a great marketplace with many **vendors**. They sold ripe, delicious produce as well as tender meats, brightly colored fabrics and clothes, **handcrafted** pottery, sparkling jewelry, and much more.

As they rode their donkey through the marketplace, Tunde turned to his son and said, "I wonder what we will learn today."

Soon a crowd gathered around them, and the people stared and laughed at Tunde and his son riding on their donkey. Tunde and Usman were confused, as the people talked and pointed at them.

"Look there!" one of the people shouted. "A man and his son riding a donkey. Has the old man no heart? That donkey looks tired and they continue to sit on its back."

Another person yelled, "That donkey is being **mistreated**."

When Tunde heard the people's comments he said to his son, "We are learning things already. If we had not left our village, we would have never known that we were mistreating our donkey." So Tunde jumped off of the donkey and began to walk next to it, leaving his son to ride on the donkey.

They continued to travel for many days until they found another large village. Tunde turned to Usman and said, "I wonder what we will learn today, son."

But again a crowd of people gathered around them. Again the people pointed and some of them said, "I cannot believe my eyes!

Guided Reading:

> **1.** *What happens first in the passage?*

> **2.** *What happens next in the passage?*

The tired old man walks while the child rides on the donkey's back. Does the child have no respect for his father?"

Tunde listened to the people's comments and became very confused. He said to Usman, "We are learning so much about the world. You must walk while I ride the donkey." So Tunde and his son exchanged places, and they left the village with Tunde on the donkey and Usman walking.

Many days later, they entered a third, very large village—the biggest one so far. The village was not in the lush rain forest like the previous two; it was in the middle of a sandy plain on the edge of a great desert. Most of the men wore flowing white garments.

"Son, I wonder what we will learn today in this wonderful village," Tunde said.

But again the donkey grew a great crowd, and again the people laughed and stared at the boy walking and the old man riding the donkey. Some people exclaimed, "Can you believe a father would make his son walk while he rides in comfort? All fathers should think about their children before themselves."

Tunde and Usman grew very confused by the people's words. Tunde said, "Son, we learn new things every day, and we should not be riding the donkey, but should be walking to preserve the donkey's strength." They left this village, both walking along side the donkey.

Soon they came to a fourth village. The people were dressed elegantly and rode camels. "I wonder what we will learn today," Usman said.

Again the people gathered around them, staring and pointing and saying, "Are this man and his son out of their minds? They are tired from walking, yet they do not ride their donkey. The sun's heat must have driven them **insane**."

Tunde listened to the comments, and he thought for a long time. "It is time to go home, son," he said. "We have learned a great deal on our visits to these villages. Jump back on the donkey, and we will both ride on the donkey as we did when we began our journey."

Tunde and Usman climbed on the donkey and started back toward their village.

Tunde leaned down toward Usman and said, "You can learn a lot about the world by listening; but in the end you must always use common sense and do what you think is right."

Guided Reading:

3. *What is the problem in the passage?*

4. *How is the problem solved?*

Name _____ Date _____

◄ INDEPENDENT PRACTICE: Checking Comprehension

Circle the best answer for items 1–4. For item 5, write your answer in complete sentences on the lines provided.

1. What is the passage mostly about?
   A. A father teaching his son how to travel
   B. A son moving his father to another village
   C. A man and his son on a journey to learn new things
   D. A man and his father learning how to care for a donkey

2. In the first village Tunde and Usman learn that the villagers —
   A. have a lot of different beliefs
   B. believe they are mistreating the donkey
   C. think there are many lessons to learn
   D. disagree that the world is very big

3. Why are Tunde and Usman confused?
   A. Every village believes something different.
   B. Every village wants the father and son to live there.
   C. They cannot find their way home.
   D. Every village is the same.

4. Tunde gets off the donkey so that only his son is riding it because the people of one village —
   A. tell him not to ride the donkey
   B. think that he is too proud to walk
   C. believe that riding on the donkey brings bad luck
   D. said that he and Usman were mistreating the donkey

5. Why do you think that Tunde decides that "it is time to go home"?

   _____

   _____

   _____

   _____

◀ BUILDING VOCABULARY: Using Prefixes

A prefix is a set of letters that can be added to the beginning of some words. Adding a prefix changes the word's meaning.

The prefix *mis-* means "bad" or "wrong."

mis-	
Examples	**Meanings**
mistreated	treated badly
misused	used incorrectly

The following words have the prefix *mis-*. Write the correct word to complete each sentence.

misbehaved	misplaced	misspelled
miscounted	misread	misunderstood

1. The mail carrier _____ the address, so the letter got lost.

2. I had _____ Mississippi when I wrote the address on the envelope.

3. Cindy did not get dessert because she _____ during dinner.

4. There were eleven kittens, not eight. We had _____ them the first time!

5. He couldn't find the dictionary because he had _____ it.

6. I _____ what the teacher said, and I went to the library at nine.

◀ LESSON 12: Understanding Characters

Understanding characters in a story or novel helps your overall understanding of the writing. It also helps you to predict what will happen in the story.

A character is a person, animal, or made-up creature that is part of a story's action. To understand a character, think about the character's traits and motivations. Think about the conflicts or problems that character has. Individual qualities such as being honest and trusting as well as things such as behavior and appearance are the character's traits. A character's motivations are the reasons why the character does what he or she does.

There are other things to notice about characters. The character's point of view is how the character understands and feels about what happens in the story. Character relationships are the connections between two or more characters, such as how they get along together.

Read the paragraph below. Think about who the main character is and what he or she is like.

> I was still a little girl when my dad gave me my first pair of skates and began taking me to the ice rink on weekends. At first, we just skated around the rink in big circles. I practiced every weekend and could soon do figure eights on each foot. As I got better, Dad helped me skate backward and taught me how to stop and turn quickly. Because of all the time Dad spent with me at the rink, I was soon known as the best skater in our town. My dad was a hockey player when he was younger, and he hoped that I would be one, too. So when I turned six, he gave me my first hockey stick. The first time I slapped a puck into the net, I felt the most incredible thrill in the world. To this day, every time I lace up my skates, I think of Dad and those Saturdays we spent together.

Name _____ Date _____

Think about the characters in the paragraph. Underline details about one of them in one color. Underline details about the other character in another color.

Choose one of the characters in the passage. Write his or her name in the oval below. Then write the character's traits and an example from the passage of each in the boxes.

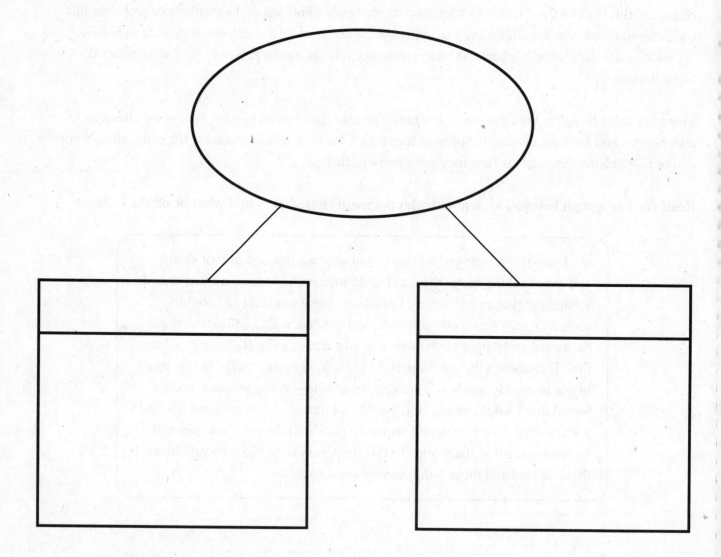

Name _____   Date _____

Read the passage. Write your answers to the boxed questions as you read to check your understanding.

Like Father, Like Son

Lloyd watched his son intently. His fears of Garrett getting injured were always floating in the back of his mind, but he knew that Garrett was very good at keeping safe and not overextending himself. He watched as Garrett rode the half-pipe¹ doing all the tricks he had learned since he started riding skateboards with Lloyd eight years ago. Some tricks Lloyd had taught him, and other tricks Garrett had taught himself by watching other skaters and reading *Thrasher* magazine. Lloyd new that someday Garrett would be competing all over the world in skateboard competitions.

---

1. *Who are the characters in this passage?*

Garrett knew he was one of the best skateboarders in town, but he never tried anything that would get him seriously hurt. He was a typical 12-year-old—oversized pants hanging below his hips, overly gelled hair that spiked to points all over his head, and a black System of a Down concert T-shirt. Only one thing set him apart from the other skaters: his shoes—old school, black-and-white checkered ones that he and his dad wore.

---

2. *What are Garrett's character traits?*

The skate park was overcrowded with skaters and pretenders. Lloyd sat in the bleachers feeling pride emanate from his whole body with the power of a spotlight shining high into the sky. He watched as Garrett rode the vert ramp like a pro and did one trick after another. "He is an awesome skater," Lloyd thought. "I was never this good."

At age 12, Lloyd and his best friend and neighbor, Kevin, were both established skaters, but Kevin was a little better. They had the same skateboards. The only way to differentiate between the two boards was the wheels—Kevin's were neon orange, while Lloyd's were neon green. Kevin's dad had built a ramp that was about four feet in height, sloping steadily from the ground to the top edge of the ramp. Every day, Kevin and Lloyd would ride the ramp, taking turns and teaching each other new tricks. Kevin always knew

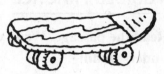

all of the tricks and learned them much faster than Lloyd. Eventually, Kevin became so skilled at riding a ramp that he began entering competitions and doing very well. Soon after this Kevin and Lloyd found new friends, and they ultimately lost touch altogether.

Remembering Kevin, the ramp, and being 12 years old brought back many memories for Lloyd. He regretted not following the same road Kevin had. He wished he were 12 years old again so he could get out there and start riding like other skaters.

"Dad," yelled Garrett, "Watch this!"

Garrett was just beginning his second time on the vert ramp. He had just perfected a new trick: the beni-hana.[2] He began with a few basic tricks, then it was time. He got speed down the vert of the ramp and took off of the other side with a lot of air like a rocket soaring up into outer space. He flawlessly completed the trick, landing with his hand pumping into the air like he had just won the biggest race of his life.

Lloyd was very proud. In his mind, he could still see the bottom of Garrett's skateboard—the image of an eagle. Garrett was graceful when riding the skateboard and was strong in his values and ideals regarding his love of skateboarding. That was the moment that Lloyd knew he had succeeded as a father. He had passed on his love of skateboarding, but Garrett had taken it a step further. Garrett was a confident and successful young man, and based on this moment, Lloyd would forever be proud of his son.

Lloyd was deep into his own thoughts when he was startled out of his daydream by someone yelling his name. Other skaters were egging Lloyd on to come and ride.

---

3. *What is Lloyd's relationship with Garrett?*

"Dad! Dad!" Garrett was screaming at the top of his lungs. "Come on! Grab your board and show us some of your old school tricks."

A smile slowly appeared on Lloyd's face. He reached down and grabbed his board—the same board he had used when he was 12—an antique, over 20 years old. He was going to show these young kids a thing or two about skateboarding!

[1] a ramp with a flat bottom and a curved section that leads to two vertical sides; also called a vert ramp

[2] a grab in which the front foot pulls the board as far forward as possible, leaving the back foot to hang in the air, and the back hand grabs the tail of the skateboard before pulling it back under the skateboarder's feet

◀ INDEPENDENT PRACTICE: Previewing Vocabulary

The words in the Word Bank are from the passage you are about to read. Study the definitions. Complete the activity that follows to get familiar with the words before you begin reading. Write the correct word to complete each sentence.

Word Bank
headstrong — determined to have one's way
stubborn — unwilling to change or give in
extravagant — willing to pay more than something is worth
jeered — spoke or shouted in a mocking way
contrary — marked by stubborn resistance to and defiance of authority or guidance

1. The _____ sailor would not go onto shore despite the fact that the captain had asked him to.

2. Grandpa Bud has always been _____, so no one was surprised by his refusal to change the color of his house.

3. We paid an _____ amount to get the beautiful table.

4. Jake was _____, so he built the model the way he wanted to.

5. The unpleasant fans _____ as the opposing team ran onto the field.

Name _____ Date _____

Read the passage. As you read, answer the guided reading questions on your own paper.

Matti and Liisa

When Matti married Liisa, he thought she was the most pleasant woman in the world. But soon Liisa began to show that she was as **headstrong** as a goat and set on having her own way.

Matti had been taught that a husband should be the head of his family, so he tried to make Liisa obey. But this didn't work. It only made Liisa all the more **stubborn**.

Every time Matti asked Liisa to do one thing, she was bound to do the opposite, and work as he would, she generally got her way in the end. Although Matti's friends made fun of him, he was a patient sort of man who put up with Liisa's ways as best he could. So Matti and Liisa managed to live life fairly well.

One year as harvest time came around, Matti thought to himself, "I am a jolly goodhearted fellow who likes a bit of company. If only I had a pleasant sort of wife! It would be a fine thing to invite all our friends to the house and have a nice dinner and a good time. But it's no good thinking of it, for as sure as I propose a feast, Liisa will declare a fast." Just then a happy thought struck him and Matti smiled. "I'll get the better of Liisa. I'll let on I want to be quiet, and then she'll want the house full of guests."

A few days later Matti said, "The harvest holidays will be here soon, but don't you go making any sweet cakes this year. We're too poor for that sort of thing."

"Poor! What are you talking about?" Liisa snapped. "We've never been more wealthy than we are this year. I certainly will bake a cake, and a good big one, too."

"It works," thought Matti. "It works!" But he only said, "Well, if you make a cake, we won't need pudding, too. We mustn't be wasteful."

"Wasteful, indeed!" Liisa grumbled. "We shall have pudding and a big cake!"

Matti pretended to sigh, and rolled his eyes. "Pudding's bad enough, but if you take it in your head to serve stuffed pig again, we'll be ruined!"

Guided Reading:

1. *Who are the characters in the passage?*

2. *Think about Matti and Liisa's actions, words, and thoughts up to this point of the story. If this is all you knew about their character, how would you describe their personalities?*

3. *Has your judgment of Matti's personality changed from how you responded to item 2 above?*

"You'll butcher our best pig," said Liisa, "and let's hear no more about it."

"But our fine apple cider," Matti went on. "Promise me you won't open a single jug. We've barely enough to last us through the winter as it is."

Liisa stamped her foot. "Are you crazy, man? Who ever heard of stuffed pig without apple cider! We'll have apple cider and coffee. Don't you call me **extravagant**!"

"Oh dear, oh dear," Matti sighed. "If you're going to invite a lot of guests, on top of everything else, that'll be the end of it. We can't possibly have guests."

"And have all the food spoil with no one to eat it, I suppose?" **jeered** Liisa. "Guests we'll have, and what's more, you'll sit at the head of the table whether you like it or not."

"Well, at any rate, I won't drink any apple cider," said Matti, growing bolder. "If I don't drink, the others won't, and then we'll have that cider through the winter."

Liisa turned on him, furious. "You'll drink with your guests as a host should, till every last jug is empty. There! Now will you be quiet?"

When the day arrived, the guests came, and great was the feasting. They shouted and sang round the table. Matti made more noise than any one else. So much so, that Liisa suspected that she had been tricked. It made her furious to see him so jolly.

As time went on, Liisa grew more and more **contrary**. There was no living with her! Then on one spring day, when all the streams were high, Matti and Liisa were crossing the wooden bridge over a little river near a meadow. Matti crossed first and noticed that the boards were badly rotted. He called out without thinking, "Look where you step, Liisa. The plank is rotten there. Go lightly or you'll break through."

"Step lightly!" shouted Liisa. "I'll do as—"

But for once Liisa didn't finish what she had to say. She jumped heavily with all her weight on the rotted timbers and fell into the swollen stream.

Matti thought for a moment and then ran upstream as fast as he could go. "I should be searching downstream, not up," he thought. "But my Liisa is bound to go against the current!"

Guided Reading:

4. *Which character trait does Liisa show when she plans the feast?*

◀ INDEPENDENT PRACTICE: Checking Comprehension

Circle the best answer for items 1–4. For item 5, write your answer in complete sentences on the lines provided.

1. To convince Liisa to have a harvest holiday feast, Matti —
   A. marries her quickly
   B. waits and plans for one year
   C. leads her across a rotten bridge
   D. tricks her into doing what he wants

2. Liisa plans the harvest holiday feast because she —
   A. is in a very good mood
   B. decides which friends of Matti's to invite
   C. always does the opposite of what Matti wants
   D. wants to make up her own mind about what to cook

3. Why does Matti trick Liisa?
   A. He wants to have company over.
   B. His friends want to visit him.
   C. He is feeling hungry.
   D. He loves his wife.

4. Why does Liisa jump on the bridge?
   A. She is angry about being tricked.
   B. Matti asks her to marry him.
   C. She is in a hurry to get home.
   D. Matti tells her to be careful.

5. Describe the relationship between Matti and Liisa.

   _____

   _____

   _____

   _____

Name _____ Date _____

◀ BUILDING VOCABULARY: Using Antonyms

Antonyms are pairs of words that have opposite or nearly opposite meanings. *Good–bad* and *happy–sad* are examples of antonyms. When you are trying to figure out the meaning of an unfamiliar word, check to see if a word with an obviously opposite meaning is nearby. Look at the underlined antonyms in this sentence.

"I should be searching <u>downstream</u>, not <u>up</u>," he thought.

Knowing what *up* means helps you understand the meaning of *downstream*.

Match the words in the box with the antonyms below. Write each word on the line.

hopefulness	fast	criticize	heavy	stubborn
dullness	transfer	headstrong	wealthy	preference

1. light _____

2. keep _____

3. feast _____

4. poor _____

5. dislike _____

6. easygoing _____

7. willing _____

8. encourage _____

9. brilliance _____

10. discouragement _____

Use each pair of antonyms in a sentence.

11. scowl, smile

_____

12. cause, effect

_____

◀ LESSON 13: Using Text Features

Books and passages are organized to help you understand their meaning. The ways in which authors organize books and passages can help a reader locate information. *Tables of contents*, *graphic features*, and *headings* are three methods authors use to present and organize information in books and passages.

Using text features can help you do the following:
• Understand the information in the text more easily and quickly
• Identify the most important ideas
• Understand the author's purpose for writing
• Understand how the author organized the writing

Graphic features such as pictures, maps, and charts help readers locate information in a passage. They show specific information from a passage or new related information. Captions tell about maps and illustrations. They give additional information.

Headings help readers locate information in a passage. Headings can be a word or phrase that indicates what the following paragraph or paragraphs are about. Readers use headings and subheadings to locate information. A subheading comes after a heading. It might give more details about the information to come.

Name _____ Date _____

A **Table of Contents** helps readers locate information in a book.

Animals of the World
Table of Contents

Chapter	Title	Page Numbers
1	Africa	5
2	Antarctica	10
3	Asia	15
4	Australia	20
5	Europe	25
6	North America	30
7	South America	35

1. How do text features help writers?

_____

2. How do they help readers?

_____

Using Text Features
Reading Intervention, Grade 6

Name _____ Date _____

Read the passage. Write your answers to the boxed questions as you read to check your understanding.

---

1. *Scan the passage before you start reading it. Name the text features that the author included.*

The Thorny Devil

Where They Live

Thorny devils are lizards that can be found in Australia. They like areas that are sandy. They can also be found in rocky areas.

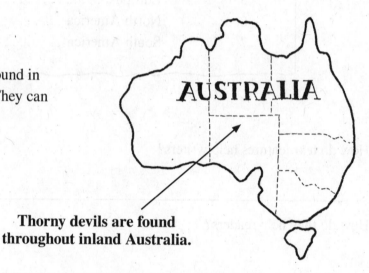

Thorny devils are found throughout inland Australia.

---

2. *Why does the author include a map?*

What They Look Like

As their name suggests, thorny devils have thorny spines. These spines are used for protection. Thorny devils can change color. When they are warm and active, they are yellow and red. When they are frightened or cold, they are a dark olive color. Female thorny devils are usually bigger than the males. Females can be more than four inches long; males are usually under four inches long.

What They Eat

   Thorny devils like to eat one thing: ants. These lizards can eat up to 45 ants in one minute. In one meal a thorny devil may eat up to 2,500 ants.

Other Things a Thorny Devil Might Eat
stones
sticks
tiny insect eggs

3. *Which text feature can you use to locate what other things a thorny devil might eat?*

How They Move

   Thorny devils move very little during the coldest winter months and the hottest summer months. But when they do move, they walk slowly. Sometimes they freeze in place. This is a way of protecting themselves.

4. *Which text feature helps you locate information about what thorny devils look like?*

◀ INDEPENDENT PRACTICE: Previewing Vocabulary

The words in the Word Bank are from the passage you are about to read. Study the definitions. Complete the activity that follows to get familiar with the words before you begin reading. Write the word that best answers each question.

Word Bank
unconscious — not alert or conscious
cardiopulmonary — related to the heart and lungs
resuscitation — revival
circulation — the movement of blood through the body
functioning — operating or working in a certain way
medical — related to medicine
survival — continued life
compressions — presses or squeezes

1. Is blood related to **circulation** or **resuscitation**? _____

2. Is a person who does not respond described as **cardiopulmonary** or **unconscious**?

_____

3. Do **compressions** or **medical** keep the heart beating? _____

4. Does an emergency room doctor worry about the patient's **survival** or the patient's **compressions**?

_____

5. Is a problem with both the lungs and the heart known as **cardiopulmonary** or **resuscitation**?

_____

6. When an organ is not working well, does it have a problem with **resuscitation** or with **functioning**?

_____

7. Is **circulation** or **resuscitation** about waking up? _____

8. Is a broken finger a **medical** or a **survival** problem? _____

◀ INDEPENDENT PRACTICE: Reading the Passage

Read the passage. As you read, answer the guided reading questions on your own paper.

Helping to Save a Life

Section 1: Introduction

Do you know what to do if you find a person **unconscious**? What if that person is not breathing or has no pulse? That person is probably in cardiac arrest and requires CPR.

Section 1.1: Cardiopulmonary Resuscitation

What is CPR? CPR stands for **cardiopulmonary resuscitation**. CPR is administered on a person who has stopped breathing and shows no signs of **circulation** (no pulse or heartbeat can be detected). When a person's breathing and pulse stop, immediate care and attention is needed to revive the person; the longer it takes to do, the more likely the chance that death will occur. CPR helps support and prolong the **functioning** of the brain, heart, and other vital organs in the body until the paramedics, or another qualified caregiver, can arrive to give further assistance and care.

Section 1.2: Basic Life Support

Before using CPR, it is important to be familiar with the components of Basic Life Support, or BLS. These skills will give you a better chance of saving a person who is in cardiac arrest due to a heart attack, drowning, electrocution, choking, or other serious injuries. The following skills are a guide to the steps to use when attempting BLS:
- Assess/Alert/Attend
- Positioning of the victim
- Beginning *chest compressions*
- Checking the *airway*
- Administering rescue *breathing*

Section 2: Assess/Alert/Attend

You may, at some time in your life, come across an accident victim who requires help. The victim's health and/or life may depend on your reaction to the situation. Your ability to react quickly, make a prompt decision, and administer aid may help save the victim's life. When you recognize an emergency, you

Guided Reading:

1. *Scan the passage before you start reading. Based on these text features, what do you think the passage will be about?*

2. *What text features does the author use to organize Section 1?*

3. *Which heading helps you know that the first step of life support has three steps?*

should use the basic steps of *assess*, *alert*, and *attend* to gain control of the situation and begin Basic Life Support.

Whenever you recognize an emergency, you should first *assess* the situation for safety by asking yourself the following question: "Is it safe to approach the victim?" If the situation is safe, *assess* the victim's condition, make a quick evaluation of how severe the injury is, and determine the age of the victim. After assessing the condition of the victim, you or someone else should *alert* the emergency **medical** services, or EMS, immediately. Then, *attend* to the victim and provide any necessary assistance needed.

Section 3: Positioning the Victim

When beginning CPR, the victim must be lying on his or her back, on a hard surface. It may be necessary to move the victim to get him or her away from danger, or because he or she is lying facedown. But remember, do your best to do no further harm to the victim when moving him or her.

Section 4: Giving CPR

One question you may be asking yourself is, "When should I start CPR?" There are three things that should be observed before beginning CPR: 1) The victim is unresponsive when you ask "Are you all right?"; 2) The victim is not breathing; 3) There are no signs of circulation in the victim, meaning he or she is unconscious, lifeless, not moving, and the color of his or her skin is blue or ashen.

Once it is determined that CPR is necessary to give the victim a chance for **survival**, you must remember the *C-A-B's* of administering CPR: *C = Chest compressions; A = Airway; B = Breathing.*

Section 4.1: C = Chest Compressions

If the victim is not breathing, begin *chest* **compressions**. To begin *chest compressions*, place the heel of one hand on the *lower half* of the breastbone (sternum) of the victim and your other hand on top of the first. Interlock your fingers and position yourself directly above the victim's chest. Then, press down on the breastbone at least 2 inches, with your arm straight and elbows locked. Allow the chest to completely recoil before the next compression. Compress the chest at a rate of at least 100

Guided Reading:

4. *Now that you have read this section, write a good caption to go with the picture above.*

pushes per minute. Perform 30 chest compressions at this rate, which should take you about 18 seconds. Count aloud as follows while doing the compressions: "One (push down) and two (push down) and three (push down) and four (push down)... thirty (push down)."

If you are not trained in CPR, continue giving chest compressions until the victim shows signs of breathing, or until EMS arrives.

Section 4.2: A = Airway

Check to see if the victim's *airway* is clear. To do this, kneel down next to the victim. Place one of your hands on the forehead of the victim and the fingers from the other hand on the bony part of the victim's chin. Carefully tilt the victim's head back and open his or her mouth.

Section 4.3: B = Breathing (Optional)

If you have been trained in CPR and have a face shield present, after doing 30 chest compressions, open the victim's airway using the head-tilt, chin-lift method. Then, place your mouth over the victim's mouth, pinch his or her nose to prevent air from escaping, and inflate the lungs with two slow (two-second) breaths (rescue breaths). Be sure each breath is big enough to make the chest rise. Let the chest fall, then repeat the rescue breath.

After every 30 chest compressions, give two rescue breaths. After five cycles, or two minutes, recheck the victim for breathing. If the victim is still not breathing, continue CPR starting with chest compressions.

If you do not feel comfortable with mouth-to-mouth breathing (rescue breaths), just continue to do chest compressions.

Guided Reading:

> **5.** *Which text feature <u>shows</u> you how to give chest compressions to a victim?*

◄ **INDEPENDENT PRACTICE: Checking Comprehension**

Circle the best answer for items 1–4. For item 5, write your answer in complete sentences on the lines provided.

1. What types of text features does the author use to arrange the information in this passage?
   A. Headings, subheadings, pictures, and lists
   B. Table of contents and headings
   C. Only headings and subheadings
   D. Numbered steps in a process

2. You know chest compressions are part of giving CPR. What section of the passage contains information about chest compressions?
   A. Section 1
   B. Section 2
   C. Section 3
   D. Section 4

3. Why would the author include a table of contents for a book containing this passage?
   A. To indicate new information added to the book
   B. To provide definitions of words
   C. To show readers the location of specific topics
   D. To display pictures of information within the book

4. Why does the author use headings to divide the passage into sections and subsections?
   A. To provide steps in a process that readers can follow
   B. To introduce new terms and their meanings for readers
   C. To give readers things to think about so they can ask questions
   D. To show the topics of each section so the reader can find information

5. If you wanted to know more about the steps to follow when attempting Basic Life Support, how would you find this information? Explain.

   _____

   _____

   _____

Name _____ Date _____

◀ BUILDING VOCABULARY: Using Suffixes

A suffix is a set of letters that can be added to the end of some words. Adding a suffix changes the meanings of words.

The suffix -*al* means "about, related to, or distinguished by."

Example: *Carolina was always interested in* <u>medicine</u>, *so she decided to go to* <u>medical</u> *school.*

The word *medicine* can be changed to *medical* by adding the suffix -*al*.

Write the correct word to complete each sentence.

medical	removal	logical	survival

1. She used her _____ training to care for many people.

2. We shared the water to ensure our _____ until the rescue worker reached us.

3. The _____ of any object blocking a victim's airway is important before giving CPR.

4. The steps for giving CPR are placed in a very _____ order.

Add the -*al* suffix to each of the words in the box. Use each new word in a complete sentence.

fiction	music	dismiss	sensation

5. _____

6. _____

7. _____

8. _____

© HMH Supplemental Publishers Inc.
© Evans Newton, Incorporated

GLOSSARY

◀ Glossary

A

acquire — get; come to have

adverse — bad, damaging

aloft — up high above the ground

B

baiting — trying to anger someone by teasing or nagging

betrothed — promised to give in marriage; promised to marry

C

canal — a channel of water

cardiopulmonary — related to the heart and lungs

christened — given a name or dedicated to

circulation — the movement of blood through the body

compressions — presses or squeezes

contemplating — thinking seriously about something

contrary — marked by stubborn resistance to and defiance of authority or guidance

culprit — the person who is guilty of doing something

D

departed — left, went away

E

eldest — born first, oldest

enlisted — signed up to serve

equestrians — people who ride on horseback

extravagant — willing to pay more than something is worth

eyesight — ability to see

eyewitnesses — people who see something as it happens

F

fabled — told about in fables

fearless — without fear

fixed — held steady, securely placed, fastened

flammable — able to light afire easily and burn

fumes — gas or smoke that is irritating, harmful, or strong

functioning — operating or working in a certain way

G

gleaming — shining, glowing

groggily — in a sleepy and confused way

H

handcrafted — made and decorated by hand

headed — directed, was leader of

headstrong — determined to have one's way

heroism — courage and behavior like that of a hero

hostage — a prisoner used to force a person or group to do something

I

inhibited — unlikely to take action

insane — crazy; mad

introductory — providing someone with a beginning knowledge or first experience of something

isthmus — a small strip of land connecting two larger land bodies

J

jeered — spoke or shouted in a mocking way

L

landslides — soil and rock that falls off and slides down slopes

locks — water-filled chambers of a canal closed off with gates and used to change the water level

M

map — to create maps of

marsupial — a type of mammal that has an outer pouch for carrying its young

medical — related to medicine

miraculously — in an extraordinary way, as though by a miracle

mistreated — treated badly

molars — big teeth in the back of the mouth used for grinding food

monarch — a ruler such as a king or queen

N

nocturnal — active at nighttime

novices — people with little or no experience

nutritional — full of nutrients for living and growing

nutritious — containing a lot of nutrients like vitamins and minerals

O

organization — group of people working together toward a particular purpose

P

pathway — lane or passageway

perceive — to become aware of something though the senses, such as sight

pursue — to follow in order to catch

R

reminiscent — suggestive, calling to memory

resuscitation — revival

retaliation — to repay in kind, to return like for like

revelation — something that is made known or realized, especially something surprising

S

seaman — a sailor

seasoned — experienced

sensitive — able to smell, hear, taste, feel, or see very well

shrubs — plants with branches close to the ground

spectacular — marvelous

sprinted — moved rapidly or at top speed for a brief period

store — to put away and keep

stubborn — unwilling to change or give in

survival — continued life

T

terrain — ground or land

tragic — related to a tragedy

treaty — an agreement between countries or governments

U

unconscious — not alert or conscious

upright — in a vertical or straight up position

V

vendors — sellers; merchants

ventilation — the flow or change of air to keep the air fresh

W

waterway — a long body of water for boats to travel on

weeded — cleared weeds

ANSWER KEY

Answer Key

Lesson 1: Identifying the Main Idea and Details

Answers may vary. Suggested answers are provided.

1. Main idea: Scientists have many theories about why dinosaurs died out.

2. Details: Many things were occurring on Earth during that time. The climate changed completely.

Guided Practice

1. No.

2. A blimp is a light aircraft that floats high up.

3. Henri Giffard developed the first successful airship. The blimp is made of the same material as NASA spacesuits, and the pressure from the helium keeps the blimp's shape.

4. Blimps are light aircraft that float up high and for a long period of time.

5. Henri Giffard developed the first blimp. The blimp is made of spacesuit material. A blimp can fly and hover for long periods of time.

Independent Practice: Previewing Vocabulary

1. seaman
2. map
3. retaliation
4. enlisted
5. fabled
6. hostage

Independent Practice: Reading the Passage

1. Captain Cook; his achievements helped future explorers.

2. Cook's early life

3. the second voyage that Cook took

4. "All these achievements led Cook to be known as a great explorer."

Independent Practice: Checking Comprehension

1. D
2. A
3. C
4. D
5. When Cook and his crew returned to Hawaii, they were not welcome. The native Hawaiians stole Cook's ship, and he took a Hawaiian chief hostage.

Building Vocabulary: Understanding Word Relationships

1. detected
2. traversed
3. seaman
4. retaliation
5. enlist
6. hostage

Lesson 2: Making Predictions

Answer may vary. A suggested answer is provided.

Derek spends the day playing video games.

Guided Practice

Answers may vary. Suggested answers are provided.

1. She is making calls to get the property cleaned up.

2. I predict that Aunt Julia calls a television news reporter next.

3. I predict that the mayor will visit Aunt Julia.

4. My predictions were incorrect. Aunt Julia did not call a TV news reporter, and the mayor did not come visit her.

Independent Practice: Previewing Vocabulary

1. store
2. weeded
3. groggily
4. shrubs
5. culprit

Independent Practice: Reading the Passage

Answers may vary. Suggested answers are provided.

1. I predict that Grandma Ana cooks and cleans instead of taking care of the baby.

2. I predict that Grandma Ana knows the answers to the questions.

3. I predict that clothes and trash will be found in the refrigerator next.

4. I predict that the narrator will see Grandma Ana putting the wrong thing into the refrigerator.

Independent Practice: Checking Comprehension

1. B
2. D
3. A
4. C
5. *Answers may vary. Suggested answer:* The refrigerator/kitchen is most important to the conflict because that is where the majority of the mystery occurs.

Building Vocabulary: Using Antonyms

1. good guy, culprit
2. solution, mystery
3. wide-awake, groggy
4. store, display
5. kind, grim

Lesson 3: Recognizing Sequence

Answers may vary. Suggested answers are provided.

1. was born in 1910
2. joined Sisters of Loreto at age 18
3. became a nun at age 20
4. spent 1931–1948 teaching high school in Calcutta
5. started her own order of nuns in 1950
6. died in 1997

Guided Practice

1. He thought about what lightning is.
2. He decided to try hanging a metal key from a kite to test whether lightning is electricity.
3. Ben performed his test.
4. He learned that lightning is electrical current.

Independent Practice: Previewing Vocabulary

1. c
2. f
3. g
4. a
5. e
6. b
7. d

Independent Practice: Reading the Passage

1. They went around the southern tip of South America.
2. The treaty between the United States and Colombia was rejected.
3. afterward
4. in 1904
5. in 1914

Independent Practice: Checking Comprehension

1. D
2. B
3. A
4. C
5. *Answers may vary. Suggested answer:* Sailors wanted a canal to travel from the Pacific Ocean to the Atlantic Ocean. In 1903, Panama gained independence from Colombia. Later, the United States signed a treaty with Panama. Then the Panama Canal was built between 1904 and 1914.

Building Vocabulary: Using Synonyms

1. landslides
2. waterway
3. locks
4. canal
5. treaty
6. isthmus
7. terrain

Lesson 4: Comparing and Contrasting

Answers may vary. Suggested answers are provided.

1. Alligators: wide, round head. Crocodiles: pointed, narrow head.
2. Alligators: teeth fit in mouth.

   Crocodiles: teeth show outside of mouth; some live in salt water

   Both: can stay in fresh water

Guided Practice

1. green or brown color, about 2 feet long, back feet have scales
2. can run on water

3. some are green, some are brown, about 9 inches long

4. in tropical areas, bushes, trees, and rock

5. Basilisks: live in rocks near water, live in South America, run on water, scaly back feet, about 2 feet long, eat worms

   Anoles: live in bushes and houses, live in southeastern United States, about 9 inches long

   Both: live in tropical areas, live in trees, green or brown in color, eat insects and spiders

Independent Practice: Previewing Vocabulary

1. b
2. a
3. a
4. b
5. a
6. b
7. a

Independent Practice: Reading the Passage

1. The black fur is on the pandas' ears, legs, shoulders, and around their eyes. The white fur is everywhere else.

2. Pandas are different from other bears in that they do not roar or hibernate.

3. Their fur protects them from the weather. Both pandas and koalas use their claws to climb trees.

4. Pandas only eat bamboo, and koalas only eat eucalyptus leaves.

5. Both leave scent marks, and both use different types of calls.

Independent Practice: Checking Comprehension

1. B
2. A
3. B
4. B
5. *Answers may vary. Suggested response:* Pandas and koalas are very different. Pandas live in China, but koalas live in Australia. Pandas have black fur and white fur. Koalas, however, have grey fur with brown all over their body.

Building Vocabulary: Using Context Clues

1. likely
2. plant-eating animal
3. like a kangaroo
4. live only in trees
5. gum
6. honestly sharing her opinion
7. active at night
8. exactly

Lesson 5: Identifying Fact and Opinion

Answers may vary. Suggested answers are provided.

Facts: Only the glaciers in Antarctica and Greenland are bigger. There are so many glaciers in Iceland that they have changed the shape of the land. These channels fill with seawater.

Opinions: They are stunning to see. The very thought of their size is amazing. The view is marvelous and dramatic.

Guided Practice

1. It is in Pisa, Italy.

2. The tower is one of the most beautiful urban squares in the world.

3. The cause is not certain. There is a layer of water under the tower that has weakened the soil beneath the tower.

4. The last statement is an opinion. I know because whether the tower is worth saving cannot be proven as true.

5. Answers will vary but should name a fact the student finds interesting.

6. The answer to question 5 is an opinion because it's the student's opinion about what he or she finds most interesting.

Independent Practice: Previewing Vocabulary

1. tragic
2. reminiscent
3. miraculously
4. eyewitnesses
5. spectacular
6. pathway

7. flammable

8. aloft

Independent Practice: Reading the Passage

1. It was one of the most tragic and spectacular aviation accidents of all time.

2. The statement is a fact. It tells what the observer described.

3. Answers will vary.

Independent Practice: Checking Comprehension

1. D

2. C

3. A

4. B

5. The last samples of the Hindenburg's fabric were tested. The tests only showed that the fabric was highly flammable.

Building Vocabulary: Using Suffixes

1. simply

2. cowardly

3. highly

4. weekly

5. immediately

6. carefully

Lesson 6: Identifying Cause and Effect

Cause: *Tornado.*

Effect: destroyed houses, flattened areas, broken pavement

Guided Practice

1. Ice crystals form, join together, and fall.

2. They can make it difficult for people to see, cause accidents, and get people lost.

3. They become covered in snow when a lot of snow piles up as snowdrifts.

4. A small movement and hikers walking across snow can cause avalanches.

Independent Practice: Previewing Vocabulary

1. fumes

2. fixed

3. adverse

4. ventilation

5. christened

Independent Practice: Reading the Passage

1. The cost of a bridge and bad weather were the causes for the decision to build a tunnel instead of a bridge.

2. The air in the tunnel was purer than the air above ground.

3. The tunnel was named after him.

Independent Practice: Checking Comprehension

1. D

2. C

3. D

4. A

5. Since people from both New York and New Jersey needed to travel faster, the commission was created with people from those two states.

Building Vocabulary: Using Root Words

1. costly

2. finally

3. quickly

4. actually

5. automobile

6. mobility

Lesson 7: Recognizing Author's Purpose

1. Rotary Park is in bad condition. It needs to be cleaned up.

2. to persuade people to reclaim Rotary Park

Guided Practice

1. the invention of bread

2. *Answers may vary. Suggested answers:* So readers will pay more attention to the facts and information and to help them better remember the facts and information

3. To inform readers about when, where, and how bread was invented. The passage gives time periods and explanations about how bread was invented.

Independent Practice: Previewing Vocabulary

1. *Equus* is the root word for *equestrian*.

2. *Fear* is the root word for *fearless*.

3. They both mean "a beginning." One meaning of *introduce* is "to begin." *Introductory* is the adjective for beginning something.

4. *Novus* is the root word of *novice*, which refers to people who are new at something.

5. *Seasoned* is an adjective for something that has fully developed, like a good equestrian.

Independent Practice: Reading the Passage

Answers may vary. Suggested answers are provided.

1. horseback riding classes

2. In an ad. An ad is a good way to give a lot of information clearly.

2. to provide examples of positive results so people of all ages would want to take classes

3. to encourage people to sign up for riding classes at Horsing Around Riding Center

Independent Practice: Checking Comprehension

1. A

2. D

3. C

4. C

5. *Answers may vary. Suggested answer:* After reading the passage, I want to sign up for horseback riding lessons! I like how there are so many options for both beginning and advanced riders. Also, I enjoyed reading about other rider's experiences.

Building Vocabulary: Using Synonyms

1. fearless

2. seasoned

3. equestrians

4. novices

5. introductory

Lesson 8: Making Inferences

Answers may vary. Suggested answers are provided.

1. The author plays a musical instrument.

2. All the sentences in the paragraph support the inference.

Guided Practice

Answers may vary. Suggested answers are provided.

1. They need something easy to grow with good results.

2. Water is important for growth.

3. Answers will vary based on student's knowledge and experience.

4. The author does grow sunflowers.

5. The author writes about planting, growing, and fertilizing sunflowers, which I know is true and important because I have helped with gardening.

Independent Practice: Previewing Vocabulary

1. pursue

2. sprinted

3. baiting

4. contemplating

5. revelation

Independent Practice: Reading the Passage

1. Rabbit is afraid that Crocodile will eat him.

2. The crocodile will probably not go looking for Trouble again.

Independent Practice: Checking Comprehension

1. A

2. B

3. D

4. A

5. Rabbit might tell Crocodile, "I told you so." Rabbit told Crocodile not to go looking for Trouble.

Building Vocabulary: Using Root Words

1. not happy; Sentences will vary.

2. in a happy manner; Sentences will vary.

3. in a manner that is not happy; Sentences will vary.

4. state of being happy; Sentences will vary.

5. uneasy

6. easily

Lesson 9: Drawing Conclusions

1. Corals are named for the thing they look like.

2. Brain coral has tight folds that look like a brain. Divers must be careful not to touch fire coral. It

stings! Some corals are called soft coral because their skeletons are less rigid. Lettuce coral look like... well, you guess.

Guided Practice

Answers may vary. Suggested answers are provided.

1. Contact lenses require more care and have more side effects than wearing ordinary glasses.

2. The information related to discomfort, cleaning, and dry eyes support my conclusion.

Independent Practice: Previewing Vocabulary

1. inhibited
2. nutritious
3. heroism
4. organization
5. headed

Independent Practice: Reading the Passage

Answers may vary. Suggested answers are provided.

1. She was a helpful, caring person.

2. There were people in Switzerland who also had the same dedication to helping people in times of war and disaster as Clara Barton.

Independent Practice: Checking Comprehension

1. C
2. B
3. B
4. D
5. *Answers may vary. Suggested answer:* She did many things during her life. She cared for soldiers during the Civil War. Afterward, she told others about her experiences during the war. Later, she learned about the Red Cross and started a branch of it in the United Sates.

Building Vocabulary: Using Prefixes

1. unstoppable
2. independent
3. inactive
4. uncovered
5. unable
6. insane

7. incredible
8. unravel

Lesson 10: Summarizing

Answers may vary. Suggested answers are provided.

1. Hansen Gregory invented the doughnut hole.

2. Hansen Gregory, sea captain, invented doughnut hole

3. Hansen Gregory was a sea captain for a long time. He stuck a fried cake on a spoke and invented the doughnut hole.

Guided Practice

Answers may vary. Suggested answers are provided.

1. Fishermen had not caught any fish in weeks.

2. Yes. The fishermen heading back to shore and the rain are important events in the story.

3. No. This is a detail, not a main idea.

3. The fishermen are trying to catch fish, but don't catch any. It starts to rain, so they begin to go back to shore. The fish start jumping out of the water and land in the boats.

Independent Practice: Previewing Vocabulary

1. monarch
2. departed
3. perceive
4. betrothed
5. gleaming
6. eldest

Independent Practice: Reading the Passage

1. A king and his three sons

2. Each son has traveled and bought a precious thing.

3. No. These are details and not main ideas.

4. A king asks his three sons to bring him a precious thing to determine who marries a princess. Each son travels and buys a precious thing. They use the objects to rush home and save the ill princess. The youngest son marries the princess because she loves him and he saved her life.

Independent Practice: Checking Comprehension

1. C
2. B

3. D

4. A

5. *Answers will vary.* Accept all responses that name the king, his sons, and the princess as characters, how the brothers use the objects to save the princess together, and who gets to marry the princess.

Building Vocabulary: Understanding Figurative Language

1. Yes

2. No

3. No

4. Yes

5. No

6. Yes

7. Yes

8. No

Lesson 11: Understanding Plot

Answers may vary. Suggested answers are provided.

How this story started: Kent is in a bike race.

What happened next: The race begins.

What I think the problem is: Kent is nervous about riding in his first bike race.

How the problem is solved: Kent completes and wins the race.

Guided Practice

1. The woman goes from stalk to stalk, picking ears of corn.

2. Someone in the field is crying.

3. The woman finds who is crying. No ear of corn is ever forgotten or wasted.

Independent Practice: Previewing Vocabulary

1. b

2. a

3. b

4. b

5. a

Independent Practice: Reading the Passage

1. Tunde and his son begin a long journey.

2. Tunde gets off the donkey so that only his son is riding it.

3. Every village they travel to has a different opinion about who should ride the donkey.

4. Tunde and Usman make up their mind about who rides on the donkey. Both climb on the donkey and return home.

Independent Practice: Checking Comprehension

1. C

2. B

3. A

4. D

5. He realizes that different people believe different things, and he and Usman must make up their own mind.

Building Vocabulary: Using Prefixes

1. misread

2. misspelled

3. misbehaved

4. miscounted

5. misplaced

6. misunderstood

Lesson 12: Understanding Characters

Character: Dad

Trait: Patient; Example: Taught his daughter to skate

Trait: Loving; Example: Spent time with his daughter

Guided Practice

1. Lloyd, his son Garrett

2. *Answers will vary. Suggested:* confident, focused, adventurous, somewhat of a risk-taker, wears baggy clothes and spiked hair

3. *Answers will vary. Suggested:* Lloyd taught Garrett how to skateboard, feels very proud of son Garrett

Independent Practice: Previewing Vocabulary

1. contrary

2. stubborn/headstrong

3. extravagant

4. headstrong/stubborn

5. jeered

Independent Practice: Reading the Passage

1. Matti, Liisa
2. Matti is determined and patient. Liisa is stubborn.
3. Answers will vary.
4. *Answers will vary.*

Independent Practice: Checking Comprehension

1. D
2. C
3. A
4. D
5. Matti wants to be the leader of the family, but Liisa always does the opposite of what he says. Matti tricks Liisa into having the holiday feast.

Building Vocabulary: Using Antonyms

1. heavy
2. transfer
3. fast
4. wealthy
5. preference
6. headstrong/stubborn
7. stubborn/headstrong
8. criticize
9. dullness
10. hopefulness
11. Sentences will vary.
12. Sentences will vary.

Lesson 13: Understanding Text Features

1. Text features help writers organize information.
2. They help readers find information.

Guided Practice

1. headings, map, chart
2. to show where thorny devils live
3. the chart
4. the headings

Independent Practice: Previewing Vocabulary

1. circulation
2. unconscious
3. compressions
4. survival
5. cardiopulmonary
6. functioning
7. resuscitation
8. medical

Independent Practice: Reading the Passage

1. how to perform CPR
2. headings, subheadings, list
3. Section 2: Assess/Alert/Attend
4. Captions will vary.
5. the picture

Independent Practice: Checking Comprehension

1. A
2. D
3. C
4. D
5. I would read the headings and subheadings in order, starting at the beginning of the passage. When I found a heading related to basic life support, I would read that section.

Building Vocabulary: Using Suffixes

1. medical
2. survival
3. removal
4. logical
5.–8. Sentences will vary.

© HMH Supplemental Publishers Inc.
© Evans Newton, Incorporated